LIBERATED

LIBERATED

SET FREE & STAYING FREE
FROM DEMONIC STRONGHOLDS

RODNEY HOGUE

DESTINY IMAGE® PUBLISHERS, INC.

P.O. Box 310, Shippensburg, PA 17257-0310

"Promoting Inspired Lives."

This book and all other Destiny Image and Destiny Image Fiction books are available at Christian bookstores and distributors worldwide.

Cover design by Eileen Rockwell
Interior design by Terry Clifton

For more information on foreign distributors, call 717-532-3040.

Reach us on the Internet: www.destinyimage.com.

ISBN 13 TP: 978-0-7684-5074-3
ISBN 13 eBook: 978-0-7684-5075-0
ISBN 13 HC: 978-0-7684-5077-4
ISBN 13 LP: 978-0-7684-5076-7

For Worldwide Distribution, Printed in the U.S.A.

1 2 3 4 5 6 7 8 / 23 22 21 20 19

CONTENTS

INTRODUCTION

I AM ASTONISHED BY HOW MANY PEOPLE (INCLUDING Christians) are unaware that we do not inhabit but rather cohabit this planet. Many say that ignorance is bliss, but God says, *"My people are destroyed for lack of knowledge"* (Hos. 4:6). If the Body of Christ is going to walk in the full freedom that Jesus purchased at the cross, it is imperative that we begin to understand the spiritual realm that is impacting our lives every day.

The apostle Paul began to unveil the mystery of the spiritual realm to us when he wrote, *"Now concerning spiritual gifts, brethren, I do not want you to be unaware"* (1 Cor. 12:1). The word *gifts* here is not in the original Greek text. The verse should actually read, "Now concerning the *spiritual*, brethren, I do not want you to be unaware." Paul is using the gifts of the Spirit as an example of how the spirit realm functions.

Although many Christian first-world countries typically acknowledge the unseen realm on some intellectual level, many struggle to believe that the spirit world is having an impact on their daily lives. The idea that the world is inhabited by invisible beings is, to them, a metaphor or even a fairy tale like Santa Claus or the Easter Bunny. People in developing nations, on the other hand, have no problem believing in a spirit realm because the effects of demons are so overt. Witch doctors, medicine men, and voodoo priests dominate the culture to the point that nearly everyone who lives there has experienced the demonic realm firsthand.

My own American experience has convinced me that evil spirits are just as influential in first-world countries as they are in developing nations; they just manifest differently. The devil is often stealthy in how he communicates with us. If he were to make himself obvious with horns and a pitchfork, no reasonable Christian would give him the time of day. The Bible tells us that, instead, he masquerades as an "angel of light" (2 Cor. 11:14) and we are to be aware of his schemes (see 2 Cor. 2:11).

While we may not all experience physical manifestations of the demonic realm, although I would not count these out, our battle most often originates in the mind. Second Corinthians 10:3-5 says, *"For though we walk in the flesh, we do not war according to the flesh, for the weapons of our warfare are not of the flesh, but divinely powerful for the destruction of fortresses. We are destroying speculations and every lofty thing raised up against the knowledge of God, and we are taking every thought captive to the obedience of Christ."*

While the spiritual realm is very much real, it's important to remember that as we war against the invisible yet tangible realm of the Spirit, believers are fighting from victory, not for victory. The truth is that we know the end of the story in every battle we may face!

When Jesus obeyed God by dying on the cross as a man, He wrestled the keys of dominion away from the devil. That is why, when He rose from the dead, Jesus said, *"**All authority** has been* *given to Me in heaven and on earth. Go therefore and make disciples of all the nations"* (Matt. 28:18-19). Jesus restored our original commission to rule the earth.

If Jesus has all authority, that would mean that satan has none! We are in Christ. Therefore, we carry His authority into every circumstance, every geographic location, and every situation. The only way that satan has authority is when we give it to him. Understanding how to maintain our spiritual authority in Christ, to dispel demons and dispatch angels, can be the difference between becoming a captive of some evil scheme or living a joy-filled life!

May I remind you that your battle is not simply to establish your faith, but it is also to demonstrate light on the earth! The goodness of God is overwhelming evil, truth is overcoming lies, and it is the power of the Spirit that is displacing the powers of darkness! As you read this book, my prayer is that your steps would be strong, your path would be illuminated, and your sight would be made clear so that every advancement will be accomplished with great confidence! Let us apprehend our call as sons and daughters to rule and reign with the authority and inheritance that Jesus gave us!

KRIS VALLOTTON
Leader, Bethel Church, Redding, CA
Co-Founder of Bethel School of Supernatural Ministry
Author of twelve books, including *The Supernatural Ways of Royalty, Heavy Rain,* and *Poverty, Riches and Wealth*

FOREWORD

I HAVE HAD DR. RODNEY HOGUE TEACH AT MY GLOBAL School of Supernatural Ministry for many years on the subject of deliverance. I had several people in the past teach at our four-day Empowered Schools on the subject of deliverance, but once I heard Dr. Hogue speak and saw the impact he had on the students, I never asked anyone else to teach on deliverance at these schools. I have known Dr. Hogue for many years; both he and I had Baptist training and years of pastoring in Baptist churches. He was also in the first group of Randy Clark Scholars doctor of ministry program at United Theological seminary. He did his thesis on deliverance ministry. He is one of the mentors for the Christian Healing Certification Program, mentoring the deliverance courses. And he is one of the professors at Global Awakening Theological *Seminary,* where he teaches on deliverance. I have nothing but the highest regard for Rodney as a person, as a minister of deliverance, as a minister of the gospel, as a professor. He has also traveled with me to other countries where he has had the opportunity to teach on deliverance in some of their largest churches. I count him among my closest friends and inner circles of advisors for the educating and training programs of Global Awakening, my ministry.

I am so glad that Dr. Hogue has completed his book on deliverance. I believe it will be one of the "go to" books for pastors, leaders, and Christians who want to know how to help others get free from bondage and captivity. I have heard Rodney lecture on these subjects many times, and I know you will be greatly blessed by the wisdom and biblical instruction you will receive in *Liberated*.

There are deliverance ministries that see all problems and sickness as caused by demons. I don't recommend these types of ministries, feeling they are not balanced, biblical, or pastorally helpful. I am glad to be able to highly recommend this amazing book, as well as its amazing author. He is not an ivory tower theologian who has no experience in the subject of deliverance, but one who has applied his principles, practices, and *His* power and authority in the actual ministry of deliverance. Dr. Hogue has trained thousands in deliverance to help others.

One of the most important aspects of Rodney's teaching on deliverance, which is represented in *Liberated*, is the aftercare of those who have been delivered. Rodney addresses how to help people remain not only free, but grow into the potential for their lives to fulfill their destinies now that they are free.

May *Liberated* be to the Protestant churches what Neil Lozano's book *Unbound* has been to the Roman Catholic Church community. I personally know no one in the English-speaking world who could write more authoritatively on deliverance than Rodney. Buy it, read it, and put it in your library to refer back to when the need arises.

RANDY CLARK, D. MIN.
Overseer of the Apostolic Network of Global
Awakening, Founder of Global Awakening,
President of Global Awakening Theological Seminary

INTRODUCTION

*You know of Jesus of Nazareth, how God anointed Him
with the Holy Spirit and with power, and how He went
about doing good and healing all who were oppressed
by the devil, for God was with Him* (Acts 10:38).

ACTS 10:38 SUMS UP JESUS' ACTIONS ON THIS EARTH. HE
devoted much time to removing the constraints that imprisoned
and disabled people so that they could fulfill their destiny. Much of
that work included, literally, ridding people of demons.

It wasn't long after I began pastoring that I realized that same
ministry of Jesus continues through us as we help individuals
overcome their constraints and assist them into spiritual maturity. Advancing the Kingdom of God requires bringing the rule of
heaven to people's lives, empowering them to throw off worldly and
demonic entanglements, and equipping them to live in true freedom. Moving forward means addressing those constraints and, with
some, removing demonic oppression.

But getting free is one thing and staying free is another. For
many, getting free is an actual event where demonic attachments

are removed from the person. Staying free and living in freedom is a process of reclaiming what now rightfully belongs to the Lord and where the Lordship of Jesus is brought into every area of that person's life.

What started me down this road was my own personal deliverance from demonic bondage in 1981. Several motivating factors hold me to this journey of freedom and seeing others set free. First, I have personally experienced the humiliation and shame the enemy can cause, so in helping others get free there is a sense of payback, of holy retribution for past damages. Second is the joy that comes when a person is set free. I never tire of seeing the look of freedom on a person's face. But most of all, it is a love issue. In my love relationship with the Lord I want to please Him by doing my part to advance the Kingdom of God on this earth, and doing so means His army must become healthy and well-armed.

Not everyone wants to confront the demonic, but based on Jesus' example it should be normal Christianity. Deliverance is not for a chosen few or a few called. Every believer is called to advance the Kingdom of God, and in that advancement you will confront the darkness. It really isn't optional. You are in the midst of a spiritual war whether you like it or not. Either you will be a victim or you will reign as victor. My personal prayer is that you decide to overcome the darkness and live victoriously, bringing others into freedom as well.

Because getting free and staying free are two related but separate topics, I have divided this book into two sections. The first part describes and analyzes the ministry of freedom, or setting captives free. This section is written to every person who answers the call to bring Christians into freedom. My goal is to equip you to lead others into freedom in a way that honors them and honors the Lord.

I don't give you steps to freedom but rather the foundational principles necessary to minister freedom in a way that works.

The second half of the book is written to the person who wants to stay free. In this section I provide action steps that will build a stronghold of righteousness in your life that, once in place, will help you live free. You are called to victorious living. You need to be equipped to overcome. Jesus said in John 14:30, "I will not speak much more with you, for the ruler of the world is coming, and he has nothing in Me." There was no legitimate place the devil could claim in Jesus' life.

The Lord wants you to be able to make that same declaration. Is that possible? It doesn't matter if it is possible. It should be your pursuit.

Part 1

GETTING FREE

Chapter 1

MY PERSONAL JOURNEY

SOMETIMES THE MOST INNOCENT ENDEAVOR SPARKS A CHAIN reaction that is like a bomb going off in your life. When that happens it must be God, and that is what happened to me in the fall of 1981 when I attended a field education class at Southwestern Baptist Theological Seminary in Ft. Worth, Texas. I expected to be stretched and to learn a few things that would be helpful to my pastoral responsibilities. I never imagined that so casual a choice would bring me face to face with a reality that challenged almost everything I believed about being a Christian and, as a result, redirected the course of my life and ministry.

I had intentionally chosen that particular class because I knew the pastor who taught that semester. The innovative things he was doing to reach people synced with my own passions. The course was everything I hoped and I was enjoying not only the class but getting to know this man for whom I had much respect. I hung around after class, striking up conversations with him whenever possible.

One evening he said, "Today we ministered to three people who were demonized."

That really intrigued me because I didn't think I had ever encountered a demonized person. Later, when I became more educated on the topic, I realized I had experienced such encounters, I just didn't recognize them for what they were. I prepared myself to engage in a fascinating conversation until his next words.

"Two of those people were Christians."

I couldn't have said why back then, but I did not like that comment at all. It made me extremely uncomfortable. I immediately thought, *I don't believe that.* Now, I had no theology about Christians and demons. The topic had never entered my mind as far as I knew. Nevertheless, I was confident that I didn't believe what I had just heard.

The discomfort deepened and, abandoning all my former fascination, I just wanted to get out of there. Fast. I couldn't wait to excuse myself. I wiggled my way out of the rest of that conversation and quickly got back in my car to drive home.

I replayed the conversation over and over as I drove. I couldn't shake his words or the inner anxiety they aroused. About halfway home the Holy Spirit spoke so clearly it could have been audible, "Rodney, that's what you have." I'd like to say I didn't know what He meant but I did. Holy Spirit had just told me that I, a Christian pastor, had a demon.

Righteous anger swept through me and without any forethought I screamed, "You have no right to me! Leave me!" At that moment I *felt* something leave.

Then I thought, *Oh no! I have just had an experience I don't believe in!* I was in shock. I determined not to tell anyone what had just happened until I could figure out exactly what *had* happened. I never told that pastor and I didn't tell my wife for months.

Rarely do we recognize the pivotal moments of our life when they happen and this was no exception. It was only months later when I began to understand that God had engineered that night's events so that He could set my feet upon a path that would bring an incredible freedom and healing not just to myself, but to many others as well. I am convinced that we don't so much choose deliverance as it chooses us.

That journey continued when I went to pastor a small church in 1982 in Bremerton, Washington. I never planned to incorporate deliverance into the pastoral ministry. I would have been perfectly content to enjoy my own personal freedom and not have anything more to do with it. However, after being there about six months, I began to encounter people who were demonized and, as any pastor should, I ministered to them.

In the early 1980s there were many practitioners ministering deliverance across the country but there were not a whole lot of resources available, especially in my Baptist circles. There were no seminary courses that addressed this topic. I felt like I was all alone delving into something mysterious and elusive until I met a few charismatic Baptists in Texas who walked me through some basic deliverance practices.

Most of what I learned about ministering deliverance came through trial and error. It was a journey with the Holy Spirit. I made a ton of mistakes but grew a lot through them. Eventually those practitioners began to put their experiences in writing and I continued to grow and learn. As the years went on, the Holy Spirit brought me through some major shifts in my thinking that redefined how I did deliverance. Those modifications were all interrelated and complemented each other. Some were theological and impacted my scriptural understanding. Others were methodological and changed how I approached deliverance. I want to give you a brief summary of these major shifts now, but I will explain them in greater detail throughout this book as I share my journey.

Christians Can Have Demons

I remember hearing John Wimber say, "People constantly ask me if Christians can have demons. My response is usually, 'Sure. We find them there all the time.'"

I will go into a lot more detail about this in another chapter, but this issue of Christians and demons is quite confusing, and for good reason. When the pastor told me that he ministered to Christians who had demons, my immediate reaction was that I didn't believe in that. Now, I realize that those thoughts weren't my thoughts because I didn't have a belief system in place. What would make me think that? It was an immediate reaction rather than a well-considered theology.

Personally, I believe hell has a well-practiced strategy to keep people in bondage. It is called denial. If you don't think you can have a demon, that spirit is free to wreak a lot of havoc in your life. It can safely put constraints on you that prevent you from achieving your full spiritual potential. Deception is a strategy that still works and demons are good at it. Believers who think they are beyond deception are deceived already. You don't know you have a blind spot until some light exposes it. Paul said in First Timothy 4:1, "*But the Spirit explicitly says that in later times some will fall away from the faith, paying attention to deceitful spirits and doctrines of demons.*" The point is that demons target believers. They are deceitful and want to give you an erroneous belief system. Knowing that deception is possible keeps you on edge and sharpens your discernment.

I didn't have a belief system but I did have an experience. I knew I had been set free because I felt something leave me and the fruit of freedom became evident in my life. I also knew that I was born again and seriously pursuing God. It was my personal experience that motivated me to figure out these two things I had believed were mutually exclusive. I couldn't deny that I had been in bondage and now I was free. If this is your major hang-up, please stick with me before you toss this book. Ask the Holy Spirit to give you eyes to see His truth.

Where You Do Deliverance Determines How You Do Deliverance

When I first started doing deliverance I followed what I thought was the biblical model from the gospels and the book of Acts. It was a combative approach based on my belief that the minister should exercise his God-given authority to cast the demon out whether the person was an unbeliever or a believer. I considered it was my job to cast out demons wherever I found them and, in my zeal, I was aggressive and confrontational.

Along the way I adjusted my thinking as I realized that the combative model found in the gospels and the book of Acts represents the inevitable clash of bringing the Kingdom of God into a place unfamiliar with the Kingdom. This resulted in Kingdom confrontations of all sorts. In the Kingdom invasion model, delivering individuals from the grip of the demonic was commonly confrontational and expressive as light invaded darkness. Demons might cause the person to scream or the demon might throw the person to the ground. Such manifestations were often dramatic and the person casting out the demon was necessarily forceful.

However, once a person belongs to the Kingdom of God, the process of setting him free looks very different. This model, designed to equip and empower, is found in the pastoral epistles—the writings of Paul, James, Peter, and John, where the emphasis is on cleaning up the sheep. I don't have to use the Kingdom invasion model to clean up the sheep. This is a very different process that pulls the person in as a participant rather than doing something *to* him as a spectator. It is a much more effective means of freedom and empowerment and is designed to equip the saints to walk in the light.

Here is an example of the first, or Kingdom invasion, model. If I'm traveling to see my friends in Mozambique and we go to a village where the gospel of the Kingdom hasn't been shared, the activity of sharing the gospel is going to provoke the darkness and there are going to be some manifestations, many times by the witchdoctor and others involved in witchcraft. Those manifestations can be very demonstrative and sometimes violent as two kingdoms clash. That witchdoctor may end up on the ground screaming with his or her face contorting or violently shaking as the presence of God descends on the village. Deliverance happens as believers exercise the authority of Jesus, and often those witnessing it get an eyeful of who, exactly, is the King of Kings. Many choose to follow Christ as a result. However, once they come into the Kingdom of God, deliverance becomes a matter of cleaning up the sheep and empowering them to stay clean. How deliverance is undertaken with those new believers should reflect the difference between a Kingdom-invasion power clash and the necessary process of equipping and empowering believers.

Participation of the Person Facilitates Empowering and Maturing Them

When the person was just a spectator rather than a participant, it was all me commanding the demons to leave. I spoke to the demon to identify inroads in the person's life. Then I led the person to confess, renounce, or repent in order to close the open door of access. When all the identified inroads, or doors of access, were closed I commanded the demon to leave. In many of my sessions, the person did nothing other than cooperate with me and do what I told him to do. This produced individuals who were set free, but were not well equipped to stay free or fight their own future battles. My sole objective was expelling the demon and I didn't see a need for anything further.

Eventually this type of ministry will wear a person down. Not only did I wear out but so did my team. It was obvious something had to change. But I had been learning a lot during that time and, several years into it, I began to teach the person how to participate in his own deliverance. I quit talking to demons and started talking more to the Holy Spirit for the information I needed.

I used the ministry time as an opportunity to equip the participant, sort of like on-the-job training. Nothing about our sessions was pretend or practice. We were dealing with real demons in very authentic, face-to-face encounters. These are great teaching and coaching moments during which a person learns very quickly how to put into action his identity and his authority and how to cooperate with the Holy Spirit. The result was that those with whom we ministered grew spiritually as they were able to put their faith into action. My job as pastor wasn't to enable them but to empower them. I realized that if I didn't teach them to fight I would end up fighting their battles for them. Spiritual maturation requires believers to take personal responsibility and walk out their faith with confidence in who they are in Christ.

Always Give Priority to the Person

The deliverance session is always about the person, not the demon. As important as it is to get the demon out, you don't want to sacrifice the person to accomplish that. You must see him as an important individual whom God lavishly loves and honor him as His creation. Deliverance should be an act of love as you minister from a heart of compassion. When ministry doesn't flow from that kind of love and honor, it is possible that the person will need a deliverance from his deliverance session. Such people attend the deliverance session on Monday but go the inner healing ministry on Tuesday to recover from the shock of the previous day's deliverance.

A woman who attended our church decided to go to a free deliverance session being offered from a ministry that had a radio show. She invited some from our church to go with her. Those in our church told her that we could minister to her in that area and warned her that we didn't know these people or how they did deliverance. She went anyway but returned, somewhat traumatized, saying she should have listened to our counsel. During her ministry they went so far as to hit her lightly with the Bible to try to get the demons out.

Some deliverance ministries' sole objective is to remove the spirit regardless of the cost. However, you can't sacrifice the person on the altar of your agenda. Your objective is to love the person, not wound them. This priority shift was a major movement on my learning curve and changed how I did deliverance. In the beginning I, also, focused on getting the demon out, oblivious to the needs of the person sitting in front of me. I didn't see him as God saw him and didn't love him with His love. I had a strong passion to drive out the spirit, but doing so with compassion for the individual wasn't on my radar. The Lord had to work in me to gain His eyes for people and relate to them with honor and compassion. Doing the right thing the wrong way is still the wrong thing. The by-product is that, when I started emphasizing the Lord's heart of compassion, deliverance seemed to go smoother and faster. When people feel loved, deliverance is expedited.

As I read the gospels, I noticed that Jesus was moved with compassion (Matt. 9:36; 14:14; 15:32; 20:34; Mark 6:34; 8:2; Luke 7:13). Compassion seemed to be His primary motivator and was always present as He did ministry. Compassion comes easily to a person with a strong mercy gift. That gift was extremely low on my scale and so I considered the person more as an object in the agenda of demon removal rather than the valued child of God they were. Lack of mercy really isn't a great character trait for a pastor and the Lord wasn't shy about confronting my lack of compassion.

As my love for the Lord grew, so did my love for those God loves. His heart for people began to rise up in me and I began to see people as God does. That's compassion. I also began to realize that compassion is a primary way to know that the anointing of the Lord is present for ministry. At least it is for me. I used to think the anointing for deliverance felt like confidence or courage. Now I realize that, for me, it feels like compassion. Whenever I become aware of compassion, I know the Lord's heart is manifesting and I have His authority to do what He wants done.

Don't Neglect Aftercare

I was with my wife during the birth of all three of our sons. As tough as that event was (for her), it didn't compare to raising them. No one really believes that childbirth is the hard part and the rest is easy.

Often there is more work to do after a person comes into freedom than the process itself. Once the house has been swept clean and put into order it must be reoccupied. If not, things could potentially return and it will be worse for them than before they were set free (Matt. 12:43-45). Not only do people need to be empowered in becoming free, but they also need to be empowered to keep their freedom and live in victory.

I did my doctoral dissertation on follow-up and discipleship after a person is delivered from demonic influence. In my research I discovered that a majority of the people who participated in my studies never received any follow-up plan after their deliverance. They attended a session, their demons left, and they went home hoping everything would be fine after that. According to my surveys that worked for some, but for many, the period after deliverance was a huge struggle. It seems that post-deliverance aftercare isn't on the radar of most deliverance ministries. They see their assignment like a surgeon who removes or corrects the problem then sends the patient elsewhere for physical therapy and rehabilitation.

The deliverance minister may think he did his job by removing the demon and now it is someone else's job to provide aftercare. This mindset, that casting out demons is the extent of the ministry, is reinforced by the fact that so few individuals can obtain freedom ministry at their own church. They are forced to go somewhere else to a "specialist" to get rid of their bondage and, when they return to their church, will have no more contact with the original ministry. Rarely does a church without freedom ministry offer adequate post-deliverance care.

There is no doubt that I approach this subject as a pastor who thinks it is important to shepherd the flock. I pastored churches over 32 years so it is ingrained in me. People who grow the fastest tend to be in a committed relationship with other believers doing life together. People who grow the fastest are intentional in what they do. They have purposefully pursued an intentional process for building identity and establishing godly strongholds. When people are set free from demons, having a spiritual community and a process to follow will give them the best chances of not only staying free but excelling in victorious living! Any church can be the place that helps people not only obtain freedom but also facilitates them into living out their freedom. Hopefully, this book will motivate you to help your church become that place.

Chapter 2

AUTHORITY, POWER, AND THE NATURE OF DEMONS

I LOVE THIS STORY IN ACTS 19:13-16. A BUNCH OF JEWISH exorcists thought they found the secret formula for casting out demons until they got a rude awakening!

> *But also some of the Jewish exorcists, who went from place to place, attempted to name over those who had the evil spirits the name of the Lord Jesus, saying, "I adjure you by Jesus whom Paul preaches." Seven sons of one Sceva, a Jewish chief priest, were doing this. And the evil spirit answered and said to them, "I recognize Jesus, and I know about Paul, but who are you?" And the man, in whom was the evil spirit, leaped on them and subdued all of them and overpowered them, so that they fled out of that house naked and wounded.*

The passage goes on to say that this story traveled throughout the countryside and both Jews and Greeks were paralyzed with fear, so much so that people came disclosing their dark practices.

Some who read this passage might wonder if God will really back them up if they try to confront the demonic. Keep in mind that these guys were unbelievers. Their faith was based on the magic formula, *the name of Jesus* (whom Paul preaches about—just to clarify which Jesus they were referring to). They didn't realize Paul's authority came not from special words, but as a result of his union with Jesus. Something they lacked.

The other interesting thing is that Paul's name was known in hell. Word had traveled in the demonic realm not to mess with Paul or it might not turn out well. For me personally, I didn't think I ever wanted to be known in hell. I had hoped to stay under the radar so the kingdom of darkness would ignore me. But this is a deception because the kingdom of darkness never ignores a saint. The truth is, whenever you start advancing the Kingdom of God, word will travel in both kingdoms. You may gain a reputation in hell like Paul, but you are also gaining a reputation in heaven!

The Superiority of the Kingdom of God

The New Testament tells us that the Kingdom of God is advancing and increasing and the kingdom of darkness is retreating. The prophet Isaiah said this of the Messiah, *"There will be no end to the increase of His government or of peace, on the throne of David and over his kingdom, to establish it and to uphold it with justice and righteousness from then on and forevermore. The zeal of the Lord of hosts will accomplish this"* (Isa. 9:7). His Kingdom is increasing, not decreasing! Hopefully your end-time theology reflects that understanding.

Jesus' rule was universally inaugurated on the cross where satan and his kingdom were stripped of all authority (Col. 2:15). Now Jesus has all rule and authority and is bringing everything under His feet (Matt. 28:18; 1 Cor. 15:24-28). We get to participate, being

His hands and feet as He exercises His rule on the earth. Today, we operate according to the same model that Jesus demonstrated to the original disciples as He showed them how to advance the Kingdom. Jesus declared the gospel of the Kingdom and then demonstrated it (Matt. 4:23). Sometimes He would demonstrate it first and then declare it. He sent His disciples out to do the same (Luke 10:1,9). Jesus then commissioned them to teach *their* disciples to do all that Jesus taught them (Matt. 28:19-20).

The declaration of the gospel of the Kingdom is often accompanied by a demonstration of power. That power was promised not only to first-century believers but to any who believe in Jesus (John 14:12). It was a common occurrence in the book of Acts[1] because they received power when the Holy Spirit came upon them (Acts 1:8). The demonstration of power commonly accompanied Paul's preaching (1 Cor. 2:1-5; 4:20) as he said in Romans 15:19, *"in the power of signs and wonders, in the power of the Spirit; so that from Jerusalem and round about as far as Illyricum I have fully preached the gospel of Christ."* The most common power demonstrations were healing and casting out demons. It appears that there is no shortage of sick people or people in bondage. The bottom line is that if you are going to advance the Kingdom of God, you will be doing the same. This makes me think that casting out demons should be normal Christianity.

The Reality of Demons

When it comes to the demonic, one of the problems is that some people have made a doctrine out of their experience, especially those who have had very little experience with demons. The strategy of hell attempts to lure people into one of two extreme mindsets. The first is that demons are nowhere and the second is that they are everywhere. The "everywhere" extreme mindset sees a demon in just about everything. The truth is, that washing machine might not be working just because it is old, not because it has a demon. Seeing a demon everywhere becomes a problem because you've turned your attention to the darkness and are probably empowering it through your attention. On the other hand, some people don't see them at all and think they aren't around anymore as if some demonic plague killed them off during the dark ages, or they have mostly all migrated to Africa and India. OK, I'm kidding, but seeing them in the Bible and not seeing them today becomes a problem that needs explaining.

I attended a conference at a Baptist encampment where one of the speakers said he believed that demons were the New Testament's way of defining mental illness. That's a little hard to swallow, especially given the fact that much of the demonic activity had nothing to do with a person's mental health. There was the mute (Luke 11:14), the blind and mute (Matt. 12:22), and the woman who was crippled by a demonic spirit for eighteen years (Luke 13:11), none of which resulted from a brain disorder. To embrace that belief means that it was only the mentality ill people who recognized Jesus, crying out when He came near (Matt. 8:29; Mark 1:23; Luke 4:33).

There are a variety of scripture passages where Jesus directly encountered the demonic.[2] In these instances, Jesus did not treat them as some misunderstood or difficult to define force that negatively affected the mind. Jesus treated demons as living entities. He was never startled when they spoke through a demonized person (Luke 4:34). He was not shocked when they challenged Him, made statements, questioned Him, or displayed knowledge or intellect. They often recognized and declared His true identity as in Luke

8:28, *"What business do we have with each other, Jesus, Son of the Most High God?"*

When Jesus spoke of demonic activity in Matthew 12:43-45,[3] He implied that the demon was alive because it exhibited preferences of where it wanted to live. It demonstrated intelligence by wondering if the home might still be vacant and available. It communicated with other demons by finding others more wicked than itself and coaxing them to join it.[4]

The Bible doesn't talk a lot about demons, refusing to explain much about them or their origin.[5] The scriptures simply say that they are there, and as you advance the Kingdom of God you remove them from the places they aren't supposed to be. The Bible gives us just enough information to get rid of them. You don't need to try to investigate them, understand them, or chart their organizational structure. You only need to know what scripture says. God's Word is enough. Otherwise you can become intrigued with the demonic realm and risk falling into a demonic trap designed to seduce you toward darkness and away from the light. You can't become enamored with them and you certainly don't need to be interviewing them to gain information about the "dark side."

All you need to know is that the Bible describes demons as real living spiritual beings, which Jesus treated as legitimate self-conscious entities. They might have limited knowledge but possessed enough discernment to recognize the Son of God. They exist to serve the powers of darkness in opposition to God and man. They are devious, driven by extreme hatred for God and His creation, and will attempt to infiltrate any part of a person that is open to them. In order to truly fulfill the commission that Jesus gave, and still gives, His church, all you need to know is how to expel them from the places where they have taken up illegal residence or influence.

This is why you need courage and confidence to deal with demons and to exercise authority over them. You must be convinced of the absolute victory that Jesus already won over the kingdom of darkness. You cannot sit on the fence or vacillate. The demonic have a nose for fear and will try to exploit it when they smell it. To confront a demon, you must have the same attitude as Paul the apostle who said, *"For I am convinced that neither death nor life, neither angels nor demons, neither the present nor the future, nor any powers, neither height nor depth, nor anything else in all creation, will be able to separate us from the love of God that is in Christ Jesus our Lord"* (Rom. 8:38-39 NIV). This guy didn't sit on the fence vacillating about things. He was convinced! Just like Paul, you need to know beyond a shadow of a doubt that Jesus has absolute authority over the enemy. You must be certain Jesus has already won the victory.

When demons manifest in a person, the purpose is to get you to back off. Manifestation is an aggressive hostility intended to promote fear. When they do this, it is usually their last resort. It is the trump card they are holding up their sleeve. They thrive by living in secret, by living in the dark. They only manifest when they are driven against their will to the light. At that point they are out of their comfort zone and they want you to leave them alone. They manifest to scare you off and make you quit. It is a sign that they are on their way out because their future is certain! That's when you can smile and say, *"It's working!"*

Demons remind me of a fish in the ocean known as a blowfish or puffer fish. It is a medium-sized fish with a unique defense system. When challenged, they swell up like a round ball with spikes. They really aren't that big or threatening. It's an intimidation tactic to frighten other fish away. Demons use a similar strategy of fear and intimidation to make you back off. Just as the blowfish inflates when afraid, demons manifest.

Are You Convinced of Jesus' Absolute Authority?

When you are convinced that Jesus has absolute authority in heaven and on earth you will never be shaken. After the resurrection, Jesus told his disciples, *"I have been given all authority in heaven and on earth"* (Matt. 28:18 NLT). Is there any authority greater than Jesus? What government or man-made thing is greater than Jesus? When Jesus died on the cross, He gained the right to be in authority over all things. Ephesians 1 tells us, *"Now he [Jesus] is far above any ruler or authority or power or leader or anything else—not only in this world but also in the world to come. God has put all things under the authority of Christ and has made him head over all things for the benefit of the church"* (Eph. 1:21-22 NLT). "All things" means—*all things*, not "some things." Christ has absolute authority in heaven and on earth. Are you convinced of that? It is a truth that you must know down deep in your heart.

You need to be convinced that your adversaries have been stripped of all their authority. *"God stripped the spiritual rulers and powers of their authority. With the cross, he won the victory and showed the world that they were powerless"* (Col. 2:15 NCV).

This means the devil and his demons have no authority. Perhaps that needs a clarification because, for entities without authority, they sure seem to be causing a lot of trouble! In reality, their "powerlessness" has to do with being stripped of authority, not stripped of operating according to their created design. The devil and his demons are spirit beings and so they operate in the realm of the spirit. The spiritual realm is a level humanity doesn't understand. Because demons operate on an unfamiliar level, whenever you encounter them you could mistake their actions as exhibiting authority and power. They will attempt to deceive you into believing they still have power. But the simple fact is that they were created to operate in another realm, like angels. But just because they operate on the spiritual level that you don't understand doesn't mean they still have authority or they possess ruling power. Don't be fooled. Their ruling power or authority has been stripped.

Think about angels for a moment. They seem to come in a variety of shapes and sizes. Have you noted the strangeness of those winged creatures in Revelation 4—with different kinds of heads and a bunch of eyes? Angels can evidently materialize and appear as a person. Some seem to have more substance than others. They are invisible unless they want us to see them. They are designed to be self-sustaining, not having to eat or drink. There are probably angels in the room with you right now. These are some characteristics of their created design. If demons are fallen angels, they will possess some of the same characteristics inherent in their created design. Just because they can do these things doesn't mean demons have authority. They have been stripped of all authority.

If a demon moves a bottle of water across the table, that particular capability is part of its created design. The fear reaction that type of activity often produces can give that demon authority over that person. Demons have no authority on their own, so the only authority that they have is what we give them. The enemy operates on the authority that we give him as we come into agreement with his lies. Much of our struggle with the enemy isn't a struggle with the authority that darkness possesses. We struggle against the authority man has given to darkness.

To counter any fear and walk courageously, you need to agree with heaven instead of hell. You enter into agreement with hell when you believe hell's lies. You agree with heaven when you believe God's truths. Coming into agreement with heaven begins by dwelling on the bigness and greatness of God. Your time in personal worship, when you give attention to the greatness and bigness of God, will facilitate your victory. The devil has no authority except what you give him, so he uses deception and intimidation to disable you, to try to stop you from doing what you were created to do. He uses intimidation because it is cheap and it works. However, when you have a big God and a little devil, intimidation won't work.

How Big Is Your God?

That was the reason David was not intimidated by Goliath. He had a big God and Goliath was quite small in comparison to David's God. The others were intimidated by Goliath and would not go out to fight him. But David was a worshiper who lived in the presence of God. Worship focuses your eyes on God so that the more you gaze into Him, the bigger He gets. When David walked out to the battlefield, he basically responded to Goliath's intimidation tactics with, "Buddy, you have messed with the wrong God! It's not going to turn out very well for you today!" When you are consumed with the bigness of God, everything is relative to His bigness!

Genuine worshipers, aware of a big God, cannot be intimidated. They are too fascinated with Jesus. Warfare gains perspective when your eyes are on the greatness, the majesty, and the splendor of Jesus. Your intimacy with the King of Kings makes you intimidating to the kingdom of darkness because as you behold Him you are transformed, becoming like the one who fills your vision (2 Cor. 3:18). Gazing into the face of God crowds out darkness.

Jesus identified Himself as the Light of the World. That is also how He labeled us in Matthew 5:14, *"You are the light of the world."* Light displaces darkness. That means that wherever I go I displace darkness. Darkness doesn't displace light. I carry the glory of God as I am transformed from glory to glory. When I acknowledge the presence of God, darkness flees. I have to look at God not at darkness. When I have eyes on Him, I walk in His authority. If I'm watching darkness, I diminish my authority. Those who become too consumed with the power of the darkness oftentimes give their power to it. That pushes them toward fear.

Periodically when I travel to teach, someone will say to me, "I know you didn't know this...but we have some of the biggest covens of witchcraft here." That statement just empowered whatever witchcraft might live there. You just made them bigger than they are! When someone says that to me, I want to respond with, "Oh, but did you notice the size and the number of the angels with us? They are outnumbered and outmatched!"

You should be talking about who is on your side, not who is on the other side. Think about this story with Elisha and his attendant to get some real perspective.

> *Now when the attendant of the man of God had risen early and gone out, behold, an army with horses and chariots was circling the city. And his servant said to him, "Alas, my master! What shall we do?" So he answered, "Do not fear, for those who are with us are more than those who are with them." Then Elisha prayed and said, "O Lord, I pray, open his eyes that he may see." And the Lord opened the servant's eyes and he saw; and behold, the mountain was full of horses and chariots of fire all around Elisha* (2 Kings 6:15-17).

You need to remember that the ones on your side are greater because *those who are with us are more than those who are with them!* You can't become intimidated when you get around the darkness and those who are consumed by it. You can't get freaked out when you encounter witches, witch doctors, satanists, new-agers, and the like. You are designed to enforce the Kingdom of God so Jesus gets all He bought and paid for. Everywhere you go you displace darkness with light.

Jesus' Authority in the Believer

In an attempt to prevent you from walking in authority, the adversary works overtime to sow insecurity between you and Jesus and blind you to your true identity in Christ. He will keep you on an emotional treadmill, doubting your relationship with God because if you aren't sure you are His, you certainly aren't going to exercise an authority you don't think you have. You don't have to live in eternal insecurity but rather, as John writes, *"I have written this to you who believe in the name of the Son of God, so that you may know you have eternal life"* (1 John 5:13 NLT). You can be assured that when you invite Jesus into your life He will come in as you give Him sole ownership (Rom. 10:9-10,13). Your salvation is received, not earned through activity, as you give your life to Jesus and make Him King of your heart.

The invitation to give Jesus your life invokes the promise that you will become a new creature (2 Cor. 5:17). The old is gone and the new has come. In this relationship with Jesus you become united with Him as one. *"For he raised us from the dead along with Christ and seated us with him in the heavenly realms because we are united with Christ Jesus"* (Eph. 2:6 NLT). You are intertwined with Him so thoroughly that the scriptures describe you having unity with what Jesus did. You are crucified with Christ (Gal. 2:20). You died and were buried with Him (Rom. 6:1-7). You were raised with Him and are now seated with Him in the heavenlies (Eph. 2:6). Even though you weren't literally there, you are united with the One who was there. This is how complete your union with Jesus is!

Therefore, all that Jesus has is yours; you are a joint heir with Him. His power and authority are now yours. When Jesus was raised and seated in heaven, you were seated right along with Him. Your authority does not come from you; it comes from Jesus. It is His authority and now that you are in Christ—crucified with Christ, buried with Christ, raised with Christ, and seated with Christ—you stand in the most awesome position of all because of your bonding relationship of being in Christ. You are a child of the King. You are heir to all spiritual things. Whatever has been given to Christ now comes to you because Jesus Christ fully dwells within you through the presence of the Holy Spirit. You don't have to ask, "What do I have authority over?" Instead ask, "What does Jesus have authority over?"

Jude 9 says, *"But Michael the archangel, when he disputed with the devil and argued about the body of Moses, did not dare pronounce against him a railing judgment, but said, 'The Lord rebuke you!'"* There is a presumption among some that we should not directly rebuke the devil or his demons. Usually this verse is quoted to justify asking—if Michael the archangel didn't rebuke the devil directly but said, "The Lord rebuke you," who are we to rebuke the devil? Shouldn't we follow suit with saying, "The Lord rebuke you" instead?

There are some problems with that thinking. First of all, this event took place before Jesus did what He did on the cross. They were arguing over the body of Moses. No doubt the devil claimed some jurisdictional rights over the body. But Michael pulled rank by asking on whose authority he claimed Moses' body. Another issue is this: the regenerated man carries an authority that angels don't possess. The angelic are messengers and no doubt carry the authority of the one who sent them. They are fierce beings that can wage war in the heavenlies and win. On the other hand, when you come into relationship with Jesus, you have become one with the One who is seated at the right hand of the Father (Eph. 1:20; 2:6). Being united with Christ and a joint heir with Jesus, you are able to exercise His authority (Rom. 8:17). The commission in the New Testament implies that believers have the authority, in themselves, to cast out demons (Mark 16:17). If you think about it, the New Testament says that believers will judge angels (1 Cor. 6:3). Don't let the enemy undermine your confidence by watering down the authority you carry.

Do you really have a revelation of the kind of power that is working in you? Look at these verses in Ephesians 1:18-23:

> *I pray that the eyes of your heart may be enlightened, so that you will know what is the hope of His calling, what are the riches of the glory of His inheritance in the saints, and what is the surpassing greatness of His power toward us who believe. These are in accordance with the working of the strength of His might which He brought about in Christ, when He raised Him from the dead and seated Him at His right hand in the heavenly places, far above all rule and authority and power and dominion, and every name that is named, not only in this age but also in the one to come. And He put all things in subjection under His feet, and gave Him as*

*head over all things to the church, which is His body,
the fullness of Him who fills all in all.*

In verse 18 Paul wants us to understand, not just with our head but with our hearts, the hope that was given to us when God chose us, as well as the glorious blessings that will be ours together with all of God's people. He also wants our hearts to know the power that is working in us. It is the same power that raised Jesus from the dead and put Him at the right hand of the Father. How much power does it take to do that one? Think about the resurrection. It begins with an earthquake and a stone rolling away. How much power does it take to do that? Then raise a lifeless body from the dead—not just the old body like what happened to Lazarus, but a glorified resurrected body that lasts forever! Then on top of that, raise Him to the right hand of the Father to the place that is *"far above all rule and authority and power and dominion, and every name that is named, not only in this age, but also in the one to come."* How much power does it take to do that? And to think, that is the power resident within you!

You will live your life not by what you know in your head, but what you believe in your heart. If you knew that power in your heart, do you think that might make a difference in how you live? How you face obstacles, struggles, disappointments, temptation, tribulation, etc.? Jesus wants you to know the kind of power at work in you so you can come into agreement with heaven and walk in Kingdom authority. Jesus said to His disciples:

I was watching Satan fall from heaven like lightning. Behold, I have given you authority to tread on serpents and scorpions, and over all the power of the enemy, and nothing will injure you. Nevertheless do not rejoice in this, that the spirits are subject to you, but rejoice that your names are recorded in heaven (Luke 10:18-20).

Jesus didn't give you that authority just to sit around and do nothing. He didn't bring you this far to lose the battle. He didn't give you that kind of authority so you can watch someone else exercise it. You have been commissioned to expand the Kingdom of God and bring *light* everywhere you go. You need to exercise the authority you have been given.

You are in a spiritual war and it is a constant thing. You put on your spiritual armor and go out to battle every day. You have to learn to fight spiritual wars with spiritual weapons. However, never forget that the One who is in you is always greater. *"You are from God, little children, and have overcome them; because greater is He who is in you than he who is in the world"* (1 John 4:4). Knowing who you are and what you carry opens the heavens above you as light invades darkness, heaven invades earth. Your agreement with heaven empowers light and displaces darkness.

ENDNOTES

1. In Acts 2 there was demonstration of power as a noise like a mighty rushing wind went throughout the city. People gathered as tongues of fire rested on the heads of the disciples. The disciples spoke in tongues and people heard them in their own languages. It was a demonstration that was followed by Peter's message of the gospel of the Kingdom that resulted in 3,000 converts. In Acts 3 Peter and John were going up to the place to pray when they ran across a lame man who was begging. After he was healed, a crowd gathered and Peter preached the gospel and over 5,000 men not counting women and children were added to the church. The demonstration of power was common in the book of Acts (Acts 4:29-31; 8:4-8) and was a fulfillment of what Jesus said in Mark 16:15-17.

2. The demoniac at Capernaum (Mark 1:21-28; Luke 4:31-37) who cried out, *"What do we have to do with you, Jesus of Nazareth? Have you come to destroy us? I know who you are—the Holy One of God!"* (Mark 1:24 EHV); the spirit of infirmity at Simon's house (Matt. 8:14-17; Mark 1:29-34; Luke 4:38-41); the dumb man (Matt. 9:32); the blind and dumb (Matt. 12:22-23); the epileptic boy (Matt. 17:14-21; Mark 9:14-29; Luke 9:37-43); women and Mary Magdalene (Luke 8:1-3); the Gadarene demoniac (Matt. 8:28-34; Mark 5:1-20; Luke 8:26-39); the Syro-Phoenician woman's daughter (Matt. 15:21-28; Mark 7:24-30); woman with a spirit of infirmity (Luke 13:10-17).

3. *"Now when the unclean spirit goes out of a man, it passes through waterless places seeking rest, and does not find it. Then it says, 'I will return to my house from which I came'; and when it comes, it finds it unoccupied, swept, and put in order. Then it goes and takes along with it seven other spirits more wicked than itself, and they go in and live there; and the last state of that man becomes worse than the first"* (Matt. 12:43-45).

4. Peter Horrobin, *Healing Through Deliverance* (Grand Rapids, MI: Chosen, 2008), 100.

5.   Even though there isn't a whole lot information on satan and his demonic horde, we have some. Satan is presented in the Bible as a real entity having personal attributes and is taken seriously by its writers. He is an enemy of God who is able to influence individuals and their environment though he is limited in what he can do. Traditionally his origin is depicted from passages in Isaiah 14 and Ezekiel 28. In the Isaiah passage he is entitled *Lucifer* or star of the morning, who was cast down to earth after he attempted to ascend above the heavens and make himself like the Most High (Isa. 14:12-20). The Ezekiel passage refers to the king of Tyre having fallen from favor, although elements in the passage, such as having been in Eden and being an anointed cherub, indicate that it is referring to more than a mere human (Ezek. 28:11-19). The term satan means accuser and was not originally a title. The terms devil and satan refer to the same entity (Rev. 12:9; 20:2). Revelation 12:7-10 tells of a war in heaven, which satan and his angels lost and were thrown down to earth taking a third of the angelic host with them (Rev. 12:4). He is the serpent of old (12:9) and the accuser (12:10). Satan is a created being and is unequal to his Creator. He is a personal devil given distinctive personality traits "including intellect (2 Cor. 11:3; Luke 4:1f), emotions of desire (1 Tim. 3:6; cf. Isa. 14:12f), jealousy (Job 1:89), hatred (1 Pet. 4:8), anger (Rev. 12:12), and a will. The devil commands (Luke 4:3,9) and leads rebellions (Rev. 12:1-3)." Noman L. Geisler, *Baker Encyclopedia of Christian Apologetics* (Grand Rapids, Michigan: Baker Books, 1999), 683.

The Bible does not speak directly to the origin of demons but many conclude that demons are the fallen angels that were thrown down to earth with satan. There are some biblical references that support this view in Second Peter 2:4 and Jude 6. Other origins have also been speculated. Some would speculate that demons are disembodied spirits of inhabitants of a pre-adamic earth. This theory says that earth was inhabited prior to Adam by a race that was destroyed through some catastrophy and lost their material bodies becoming disembodied spirits who want to seize the bodies of men to use as their own. Merrill Unger (*Biblical Demonology*, Grand Rapids,

Michigan: Kregel Publications, 1994, 42-45), devotes considerable time to explaining the thinking behind this speculation but concludes that it cannot be scripturally supported as the Bible says nothing about a human race before Adam. This one is pure theory with no scriptural support. Others would believe that demons are the result of the offspring of angels and daughters of men of Genesis 6:2 prior to the flood. This latter perspective is found in the apocryphal *Book of Enoch* (Enoch 15:8-11). Though there are many who have embraced this down through the ages, it doesn't seem to fit the math for me. I don't know if the population of the earth prior to the flood could have been that huge. To think the women who engaged in that relationship could have produced what seems like billions of demons today, enough to engage the earth's current population, doesn't seem to add up to me.

These non-traditional theories are given consideration because it is difficult to believe that some of the demons we deal with were actually angels. I remember John Wimber telling a story about a deliverance session where the minister asked, *"Are there any more demons in there?"* to get the reply, *"No, we're all gone."* I haven't had that experience but my experience that I can attest to is that even though you run across some with major intelligence, some of the low-level demons seem to lack any. However, that can probably be explained by living in darkness and being void of light. At least that's my theory.

Chapter 3

DEMONIC ATTACHMENT

WHEN I WAS IN COLLEGE IN THE EARLY 1970s I WENT WITH A few of my friends to see the movie *The Exorcist*. That movie did enough to steer me away from wanting to minister to the demonized. It produced fear and apprehension. That visual picture of extreme demonic control imprinted forever on my subconscious and became my stereotype of what any person with demons would look like. At that time, I didn't understand that extreme demonic control was rare rather than typical.

The truth is that all demonic attachments are not equal. Demons operate at varying levels of influence. The worst scenario of extreme demonization is found in Mark 5 in the country of the Gadarenes.[1] On a one to ten scale, this man was definitely a ten. He was totally out of control, dwelling among tombs, breaking the shackles they used to bind him, crying out and gashing himself with stones because he was possessed by a legion of demons. This man was probably described in such detail because he was the worst case of demonization that Jesus and His disciples encountered.

His freedom demonstrated Jesus' absolute authority to displace the darkness. It revealed what is possible when light confronts darkness even in this man who changed from uncontrollable and insane to completely normal. This story reveals how freedom becomes a testimony of Jesus to share the gospel of the Kingdom. However, it is not an example of the average person who has demons.

On the lighter side, there can be demonic influence without attachment but that still induces recognizable activity. In Mark 8:31-33, Jesus foretells what is going to happen to him when religious leaders arrest Him. They will kill Him but in three days He will rise again. He stated the matter plainly but it was still difficult for the disciples to hear and receive. Peter took Jesus aside and rebuked Him for such thinking. Rebuking God is never a good thing.

Jesus turned to Peter and said, *"Get behind Me, Satan; for you are not setting your mind on God's interests, but man's"* (Mark 8:33) Jesus was addressing the source of Peter's thoughts. Those weren't Peter's thoughts but were put into his mind. That is what temptation is— entertaining thoughts that aren't ours. When satan disguises his suggestions as your thoughts and ideas, you are more likely to accept them. That is his primary deception. Peter believed those were his thoughts and so he took ownership of them. He then acted on what he thought. What a great example of the way temptation works.

Just to be clear, I don't believe demons can read your thoughts. I base that on First Corinthians 2:11, which says you cannot know another person's thoughts. That is a God power that only He gives according to His will, not a demonic ability. I also know from confronting demons that they are good at guessing what you might be thinking, but they are only guessing. One time, when a demon was leaving a person, the demon spoke through the person and threatened my little girl. The problem is that I don't have any daughters. They are guessers. They do, however, know the thoughts they have put into your mind. They also seem to sense any residue of darkness that still lingers on a person. Don't be deceived—they cannot read your mind.

Another demonized person, almost a ten on the demonization scale, was the young boy in Luke 9:38-40. The demon seized the boy and tormented him so terribly his father said, "it scarcely leaves him." This describes almost complete domination except for those few moments of sanity. Unlike the Gadarene demoniac, the boy's torment was not 24/7, but it was close. In those rare moments the boy had a semblance of normality, but most of the time he was tormented. The disciples could not cast out those demons, but Jesus did.

The rest of the demons mentioned in scripture seem to fall somewhere in the middle of the scale. The mute man in Luke 11:14 could not speak. So the demons only impacted one area—his speech. He probably lived an otherwise normal life. His situation was a far cry from the Gadarene demoniac and less than the epileptic boy. The mute and blind man in Matthew 12:22 is similar in scale. He was only impacted in these two areas and the rest of his life could be quite normal. The woman in Luke 13 was crippled for eighteen years. She couldn't straighten up. Jesus revealed her malady was caused by a demon. There is no indication that she was affected on any level except this one.

These examples show that there are different levels of demonic affliction. Therefore a person may be able to carry out his life on a normal level except he may struggle with secret sins, dominating fears, or compulsive uncontrollable behavior. That doesn't mean the whole person is taken out, just those specific areas. That was me. I lived a fairly normal life and was even active in ministry. However, there were areas of my life where I continued to struggle, hiding the battles out of shame.

I was driving home one night through my nice neighborhood when I passed a home surrounded by flashing lights and government vehicles. Apparently one of my neighbors had a meth lab in his garage. Now, I lived in a nice neighborhood. I didn't live in a drug neighborhood. It was a great place to live! Just because there was one drug house on the block didn't make it a drug-infested neighborhood. Authorities didn't have to arrest the inhabitants of all the other houses. Just the one. One bad neighbor doesn't mean all the neighbors are bad.

That is the way the demonic work in an individual life. They seek to find an inroad into the life of a person (buy some real estate). Then, once they find some property for sale, they acquire it and set up their bad business. It starts off with *one* house. Not the whole block, just one area in a person's life that is yielded—up for sale. If there are any weaknesses in the houses next to them they may draw those houses into that bad lifestyle. Having the whole block, a block where every house is a drug house, is a rare thing. The demoniac at the Gadarenes had every house in his block taken, as everything in his life was overwhelmed by demons. The guy who was blind or the woman who was bent over because of a demon had only a few houses on their block under demonic influence.

That is why a person can feel and think normally in most ways but still have one or two areas he just can't seem to control. Perhaps he has a thinking system that has been corrupted. Ungodly thought patterns lead him to do things he doesn't want to do but feels powerless to resist. Most people who struggle with demonic influence have a somewhat normal life. Their struggle is only in a few areas, or possibly only one area. You have to put aside the incorrect notion that, when demons are present, a person is totally out of control and the demons are constantly manifesting. That is the rare situation.

Mostly, demons operate solely in the few areas where they have obtained a legal right.

The term "demon possession" or "possessed by a demon" is an unfortunate translation of the original Greek language. The word "possession" implies ownership or complete domination by a demon. As previously explained, demonic influence can range from mild to total domination, so "possession" would not accurately describe most of the demonic attachments in the New Testament. The better way to interpret this would be to use the terminology "demonized" or, in cases of complete domination, "controlled by a demon."[2] In looking at the actual Greek verbiage there are several ways that the New Testament talks of having a demon. One way is to use a common verb *echo,* which means "to hold" or "to have" or "to accompany" followed by the direct object of the verb, which are the noun forms of demons, *daimonion* or *daimon* or, on one occasion, *spirit.*[3] This particular verb is the same word that is used to say that Mary was pregnant (Matt. 1:18,23), that John the Baptist had a camel hair coat (Matt. 3:4), and people had a sickness (Matt. 4:24). Matthew 5:23 says if someone *has something* (same verb) against you, leave your gift at the altar and go make it right. In reference to Mary, she possessed a baby; the baby did not possess Mary. John the Baptist possessed a coat; the coat did not possess John. People possessed a sickness, and offended people possessed an offense. It is one thing to possess a demon and another to be possessed by a demon.

The verb form, *daimonizomai,*[4] is a very broad term that would include all levels of demonic influence from mild to complete control. Rather than use the term *possessed,* a better description would be to say *to have a demon* or *be vexed by a demon.*[5] Another way the scripture describes demonic influence is found in Luke 6:18, which uses a different verb that is translated *to be troubled* with unclean spirits. Mark 1:23 and Mark 5:2 employ a preposition to say a "man with an unclean spirit." Therefore, whenever you see the term "demon possession" or "possessed by a demon," this is an interpretation. A more accurate translation is *demonization,* which means *to have a demon.* There is a big difference between having a demon and a demon having you, especially because a believer cannot be owned by the kingdom of darkness. Some prefer the term *oppressed* rather than *possessed.* Personally, I just like the term *demonized* to describe some form of demonic attachment to a person. It simply conveys that a demon is present.

Sanctification of the Believer

Now may the God of peace Himself sanctify you entirely; and may your spirit and soul and body be preserved complete, without blame at the coming of our Lord Jesus Christ (1 Thessalonians 5:23).

People are created body, soul, and spirit. The apostle Paul is not teaching an anatomy lesson. Rather, this scripture conveys the very real fact that even though man is a single unit, there are different aspects of a person's being that have different functions and yet are intertwined within the person. The spirit part of man connects and relates to God. When a person sins (and all have sinned) that person is cut off, or separated, from God. Even though that condition is described as being spiritually dead (having been cut off from God), the human spirit continues to function. When that person asks Christ to come into his life he is born again of His Spirit. God's Spirit connects with his spirit as they are joined with Jesus. *"The Spirit Himself bears witness with our spirit that we are children of God"* (Rom. 8:16 NKJV). The soul is another part of the inner man. It consists of the mind (one's capacity to think), the will (one's capacity to choose), and the emotions (one's capacity to feel). Finally, the Christian's body is the temple of the Holy Spirit, giving identity plus relating to the physical world.

At salvation every part of you—body, soul, and spirit—was fully bought and paid for by the blood of Jesus and you were redeemed. The word *redeem* means to "buy something back" or "to liberate through the payment of a price." Your spirit is fully redeemed when God's Spirit connects with your spirit. Your soul (your mind, will, and emotions) has also been redeemed. First Corinthians 2:16 says that you have the mind of Christ. Your will has been redeemed as Philippians 2:13 says that God is in you *"to will and to work for His good pleasure."* God gives you the desire and the power to do His will. Your emotions have also been redeemed. He has given you the fruit of the Holy Spirit of love, joy, peace, patience, kindness, gentleness, and so on.

What has been redeemed must be reclaimed. God's Spirit indwells your spirit, so your spirit is fully reclaimed. The soul must also be reclaimed. Paul says in Second Corinthians 4:16, *"Therefore we do not lose heart, but though our outer man is decaying, yet our inner man is being renewed day by day."* The inner man is in a process of renewal and restoration even though the body is getting older and will one day die. However, even though the body is under the curse of death because of sin, it is also redeemed in that, one day, it will be fully reclaimed. First Corinthians 15:53-54 says that the perishable puts on the imperishable and the believer will receive an eternal glorified resurrected body.

Scripture talks about salvation in the past tense, the present tense, and the future tense. The moment you came into a relationship with Jesus you were saved (past tense Eph. 2:4-5,8), you are "being saved" (1 Cor. 1:18; 2 Cor. 2:15), and one day salvation will be complete when you see Jesus face to face (Rom. 5:9-10; 13:11).

Scripture also talks about our sanctification in the past, present, and future tenses. Sanctification means to be made holy or separate. You were completely sanctified at the point you gave your heart to Jesus (past tense: 1 Cor. 6:19; 2 Peter 1:13-14). You are perfectly holy because you are joined to the One who is perfectly holy. Even though you are holy in your new and true identity, your soul is still in the process of being conformed to that holiness. You are still *becoming* who you are. Christ is in you but that doesn't mean He is "formed in you" (Gal. 4:19). You are being sanctified (present tense: 2 Cor. 7:1) and some day you will be fully sanctified (future tense: 1 Thess. 3:12-13; 5:23-24).[6] You were sanctified when you gave your heart to Christ—positional sanctification. That is your position in Christ. One day your sanctification will be complete when you see Jesus face to face. Between now and then you are to experience ongoing sanctification. What's inside you must begin to manifest in your life. Even though you are sanctified, you are still pursuing who you are. Even though you are righteous, you still pursue righteousness (1 Tim. 6:11; 2 Tim. 2:22). Although you are holy, you still pursue holiness and sanctification (Heb. 12:14). Peter says to be holy in all your behavior. You shall be holy because He is holy (1 Pet. 1:15). You pursue it until what is inside you is manifesting in your life. As you walk out your Christian life, the sanctification process requires putting off the old and putting on the new (Eph. 4:22-24). It will require you to shed remnants of the old self that may still contain elements of darkness as you bring everything under the Lordship of Jesus. Those redeemed but un-reclaimed dark places are the areas where the demonic hope to find a home. Anywhere there is darkness, even the darkness that may still be found in the believer, the devil and his demons attempt to find a place to hide and inhabit.

How Can a Christian Have a Demon?

Many Bible scholars agree that Israel taking and occupying the Promised Land, chronicled in the Old Testament, illustrates the New Testament concept of sanctification. Both are journeys to possess what God has already conferred. God had given Israel the land. It was totally theirs. God said that it was the land of promise, flowing with milk and honey. Their task was to occupy the land and, in the process, remove the inhabitants. To occupy the land meant that they had to go into the land and tear down the strongholds of the enemy one by one. Remember that the land was already theirs. Why couldn't they have just walked in and said, *Hey guys, we just wanted you to know that the land you are on is under new ownership. We are here to tell you that you have to get out because this is our land. It belongs to us. You have no right to occupy it anymore. So leave!* They found that those occupants weren't so eager to depart. They had to confront them and drive them out. Each time they had to hear from God on how to do that. They were able to successfully take the land because God had already given it to them. It belonged to them. They were to reinforce the promise and evict the squatters. They owned it and now their mission was to possess it.

Once you give your life to Jesus you fully belong to Him. You are united with Jesus and all of you belongs to Him. But just because you own something doesn't mean it is under your control. What has been gained in ownership must be possessed. It may be under your authority, but someone else might be usurping that authority. You must bring every part of your life under the authority of the new owner, Jesus. It is like purchasing a home and having some of the old owner's stuff still in the rooms. You don't let it stay. You clean it up and take it to the dump. You reclaim what has been redeemed.

In Christ you are a new creature. You have the righteousness of Jesus and have been made holy because you belong to Him. However, are there any rooms in your life that have not been fully cleaned out where some areas of darkness still remain? Are there any areas that need to come under the submission of the Lordship of Jesus Christ? One by one, these areas will need to be brought into submission. Some of these places are areas of darkness. Some are strongholds that must be torn down. Some strongholds may be held together by demonic forces that must be removed. Just as God allowed enemies to remain in the land until driven out, God may allow a stronghold in your life to remain until you address it and drive it out.

When discussing this topic of Christians having demons, one common question people ask is this one: "How can darkness and light reside in the same place?" The perception is that, if the Holy Spirit is inside a person, a demon cannot also inhabit that space. And yet every person who asks that question, believing it is an impossibility for light and dark to exist simultaneously, has sin in his life. Last I heard, sin does fit into the category of darkness. So every Christian life proves that light and darkness can and do reside in the same place. Once you have received Jesus into your life, the inner chamber of your spirit is full of the Holy Spirit. This immediately displaces any darkness that had been in your spirit. But the un-reclaimed parts in your soul can still harbor darkness. When you cooperate with evil forces and do deeds of darkness, it is apparent that the light of God in your spirit cohabits with the darkness that still exists in your partially reclaimed body and soul.

There are a couple of passages that need some clarification because some have used these as proof texts that Christians can't have demons. The first is in Second Corinthians 6. It is the most commonly used passage to argue that a Christian can't have a demon and what is usually quoted is the last part of verse 14 and the first part of verse 15—*"what fellowship has light with darkness? Or what harmony has Christ with Belial?"* Belial is a Hebrew word and is a synonym for satan or wickedness. What is usually *not* quoted is the context of the passage. Context is really important! The context is not speaking about believers having demons but believers being unequally yoked with unbelievers. Paul isn't saying it can't happen because it *was* happening and he was warning those believers. This passage is actually a caution that believers *can* become entrapped by darkness, not a proof text that darkness can't attach to a Christian. It is an admonition to steer clear of certain activities or entanglements to avoid becoming entrapped by darkness. Your body is the temple of the Holy Spirit, so treat it as such and make no compromising alliances.

The second passage that needs clarification is First Corinthians 10:21—*"You cannot drink the cup of the Lord and the cup of demons; you cannot partake of the table of the Lord and the table of demons."* Again, we must look at the context which begins in verse 14. This passage is addressing a problem among certain Corinthian believers. Even though they made a commitment to Jesus, they were still offering to idols. The context is Paul addressing idolatry amongst believers. He told them, in no uncertain terms, to flee from idolatry; converts to Jesus Christ must stop sacrificing to idols. Again, Paul isn't saying it can't happen because it *was* happening. This time he warns about the danger inherent in idol worship because it will cause demonic entanglements and attachments. It is an admonition to avoid being entrapped by demons through this compromise.

Apparently the Holy Spirit was still sticking around with these guys in Corinth even though they were participating in activities of darkness. Paul admonished them to clean up those areas of their lives so darkness could not get a foothold. Paul warned them, position yourself, *"so that no advantage would be taken of us by Satan; for we are not ignorant of his schemes"* (2 Cor. 2:11). This implies that satan wants to take advantage of you and will do so if you remain ignorant of his schemes. How far can satan go in entrapping believers? As far as you let him. Remember Peter's words to Ananias (along with his wife, Sapphira) in Acts 5:3—satan has *"filled your heart to lie to the Holy Spirit."* Apparently light and dark cohabited in these two cases.

Demons Look for Open Doors

Be angry, and yet do not sin; do not let the sun go down on your anger, and do not give the devil an opportunity (Ephesians 4:26-27).

The word *opportunity* is key to understanding what Paul is saying here. He is encouraging believers not to open any door that the devil might walk through. The word for "opportunity" (Greek: *topos*) is very common and means "place, territory, area, opportunity, power, place of operation, an area of legal control." Other translations interpret it as:

- Don't give the devil a "foothold" (NIV).
- Don't give the devil a "place" (KJV).
- Do not make "room" for the devil (NRSV).

▪ *"Do not give the devil a way to defeat you"* (NCV).

Later in this book I will examine the terminology of a "stronghold" in more depth, so this is just a brief introduction for the sake of clarity. Although it is used in Second Corinthians 10:3-5 in the negative, know that there can also be a righteous stronghold. A stronghold is a fortification for either righteousness or unrighteousness. What your adversary wants to do is gain some ground in your life from which to operate. A stronghold can be a center of operation for darkness. Strongholds aren't built overnight; they are the result of process over a period of time. It begins when you give the devil an opportunity, a "foothold" to hang on to. The devil wants a base of operations in your life. There are many things that give such an "opportunity" or "right" to operate in your life—we'll look at a few in a moment. But when you open the door, you provide such a *place* because you gave him *room*. This initial basis of operation will provide a foundation for what will later become a stronghold. And one thing is for sure—if you give the devil a foothold, he will build on the place you give him as much as you will allow. Strongholds start as footholds that you don't immediately remove.

A piton illustrates this concept. A piton is a device that mountain climbers use to go up and down mountainsides. Though there are a variety of different kinds, the most common resemble a strip of metal with a hole at one end. The mountain climber will look for cracks because the piton won't penetrate solid rock. Once they find a good crack, they will hammer the piton into it, wedging it firmly into the crack. Then the mountain climber clips his D-ring to it, effectively anchoring himself to the mountain. This is a great picture of what the enemy does. He looks for cracks. He looks for hurts, wounds, and open doors. Then he seeks to attach himself to those places. How do you remove the footholds? Address the crack, heal the wound, close the door, and then demons have nothing to hang on to. Sometimes deliverance is not about casting something out as much as it is addressing how it got there in the first place and fixing it.

Our demonic adversary wants to destroy your life. He wants you to self-destruct. Demons look for a legal "right" to attach themselves to a person. They are expert legalists, looking to take advantage of the letter of the law and take it as permission. If you grant such permission and give them an "opportunity" or "foothold" in your life through your sin, someone else's sin, or any open door, they accept that as a legal invitation. Such invitations, or open doors, become inroads into your life that, if left unresolved, will eventually result in captivity. The point, or place, of enslavement becomes a "stronghold," a fortification for darkness, a thinking system that supports lies rather than truth and provides a home for the demonic.

Even after you have given your life to Jesus, the demonic will try to hold the ground you have given over to the kingdom of darkness. These attachments may come by your choice, by your neglect, or by their deception. They must be seen as illegal squatters that have no right to the believer and must be evicted. You must reinforce what Jesus bought and paid for on the cross. Remember that the devil doesn't play by fair rules. He cheats. He is a liar, a thief, and a murderer. If he thinks he has a right he will claim it. He is a legalist and looks for loopholes. He seizes what he can.

ENDNOTES

1. Mark 5:1-5 and also found in Luke 8:27-39. Some translations translate the community as Gerasenes.

2. Merrill F. Unger, *What Demons Can Do To Saints* (Chicago, Illinois: Moody Press, 1979), 100-101.

3. The passages where the verb, ἔχω (echo) is used are found in Matthew 11:18; Mark 9:17; Luke 4:33; 7:33; 8:27; John 7:20; 8:48,52. Some of these passages are ones that accuse Jesus of having a demon.

4. Matthew 4:24; 8:16,28,33; 9:32; 12:22; 15:22; Mark 1:32; 5:15-16,18; Luke 8:36; John 10:21. This verb is commonly translated as demon possession because it means to act or be under the control of a demon. It describes the person who expresses the mind and consciousness of the demon. It does not suggest ownership but it does express that a person is vexed by a demon.

5. Merrill F. Unger, *What Demons Can Do To Saints* (Chicago, Illinois: Moody Press, 1979), 101.

6. Neil Anderson, *Victory Over the Darkness,* (Ventura, California: Regal Books), 60-61.

Chapter 4

OPEN DOORS

THE KINGDOM OF DARKNESS LOOKS FOR WHAT WE CALL "OPEN doors" to gain entrance into a life. As discussed in the previous chapter, demons are legalists in that wherever they find agreement or a loophole, they will certainly attempt to exploit it. If a person agrees with any lie of darkness, the demonic will consider that a legal contract and take full advantage. Sometimes the open door is not of your choosing; you were subjected to it involuntarily, such as when a child is exposed to darkness by his parents. Remember that the adversary comes to kill, steal, and destroy (John 10:10). He does not play fair. Demons are legalists. The good news about legalism is that when you remove the legal rights, you can force demons to vacate the premises.

Sometimes you identify demons but can't find any legal rights because the legal rights have already been removed. At these times demons are like squatters who try to remain until forced to leave. On the other hand, just because you have an open door doesn't mean there are demons present. In this chapter I will identify and describe some common open doors. It certainly isn't an exhaustive list but should give you a general idea of how the adversary works. In Appendix A, you will find sample prayers to close many of these open doors.

Habitual Sin

The most common open door is a person's involvement in habitual sin. It begins with a volitional choice. You decide to sin. You decide to do something that you know is wrong. You wouldn't do it except for the gratification involved because it appeals so strongly to the flesh. You are deceived into believing you can control the situation. At first, you can stop if you want to, but there is a false sense of control at this stage and you don't *want* to stop. You keep indulging that fleshly desire until the repetitive decision to sin eventually becomes a trap. At some point you cross an invisible threshold where the sin controls you. From that moment on, stopping is no longer an option. You are a slave to that which you have obeyed. If you get to that point, there is certainly a demonic spirit driving the desires and intent on taking you out. To break free you must remove the legal ground by confessing your sin to God. Closing that door requires sincere confession and repentance, renouncing your actions and choices, so you can receive His forgiveness.

Sexual Perversion and Pornography

Sexual perversion and pornography exploit the God-given sex drive that is part of our created design. God designed us to be sexual creatures with an inbuilt ability to enjoy and express our sexuality in the context of marriage between a man and a woman. Sexual perversion is any sexual activity of a man or a woman outside of the covenant of marriage (Rom. 1:26-27; 13:9,13; 1 Cor. 6:9-10,18; 1 Thess. 4:3; Heb. 13:4). On the other hand, to view the activity of sex within marriage as shameful, disgusting, or morally offensive is also a deviation from truth. It is an equally deceptive perversion that subjects one to demonic entrapment of a religious spirit because he has taken the "holy high ground" by looking down upon what God created for enjoyment in the context of marriage.

When a person engages in pornography, he or she is using some form of media for the purpose of sexual arousal. God gave us a sex drive. Though the sex drive itself is normal, it can easily be manipulated and exploited through fantasy. Men are stimulated visually through sight. Women can be as well but to a lesser degree. With the availability of the internet, pornography is now just a few clicks away and has become a huge problem. Women (and men to a lesser degree) can find themselves entrapped in fantasy relationships, feeding their perversion through romance novels in the same way a man might feed his fantasy through a pornographic magazine. This addiction is complicated as there are endorphins (pleasure hormones) released. Pornography pollutes one's sexuality and denigrates people into objects for personal gratification rather than as God's creation deserving honor and value.

Occult

Anytime you call on powers of the spirit world other than God's Holy Spirit, you are dabbling in the occult. The occult can be the obvious witchcraft where someone intentionally contacts spirits or uses spirit guides. It can also be much less obvious, like when children innocently play with an Ouija board. There are many types of practicing witches and covens and varying degrees even within "the craft." Some know they are worshiping the devil while others think they are just getting in touch with the spirits of the natural world and are blinded to the evil in which they have immersed themselves.

One of the strategies of hell is to desensitize a person to the depravity of darkness by portraying darkness as light, an ancient plan that still works very well. A good witch is still a witch. Seduction through lowering your defenses creates a blindness where the adversary can sneak in unaware. You can open doors if you go to a person who tells the future, like a palm reader, or use new age techniques to receive physical healing. The bottom line is that anytime you call on a spirit other than the Holy Spirit you are engaging in witchcraft. It is prohibited (Exod. 20:3-5; Lev. 19:31; 20:6-8).

Cults and False Religions

Jesus said that He is the way, the truth, and the life. No one comes to the Father except through Him (John 14:6). All roads do not lead to the same place. There are not multiple ways to know God. There is no other way to enter into a relationship with God except through the only Son of God, Jesus. Everything else is a counterfeit. These counterfeits contain enough truth to pull people in because there is power in truth, but it is mixed with untruths that will lead people astray. Any religion besides Christianity falls into the cult category and some who call themselves "Christian" may not be true Christians. There are some who embrace a "Jesus" that is not the Jesus of the New Testament but a perversion of Him, sometimes having their own set of scriptures. The apostle Paul talks about the craftiness of the adversary who preached a different Jesus (2 Cor. 11:3-4; Gal. 1:6-9). Just because a religion embraces Jesus in some form doesn't mean it is legitimate. A false religion will worship a different Jesus, multiple Jesuses, or no Jesus at all. A false religious spirit turns attention away from worshiping the one true Father through His only Son, Jesus, and toward a counterfeit religion where demons masquerade as God. Items or articles associated with these false religions can invite unwanted spirits into your home.

What often entraps people into a belief system is their culture. Their convictions may not be in their beliefs but to their family. They honor their family and their community by embracing the cultural belief system. This devotion shuts down openness to truth and leaves them spiritually blind. Coming out of the belief system can be seen as betrayal of the family and culture, so many decide to stay. A truth encounter can open their eyes to see clearly, jump-starting the escape from deception.

Substance Abuse

Drugs can open your life to demonic attachment. Though some think any drug can invite demons into a person's life, personally I'm not so sure. I've never seen a demon attached to a person because he took an aspirin or his blood pressure medicine. The drugs or substances that invite demonic spirits are the ones that your body does not need, pursuing an effect that isn't beneficial to your body. Any time you take things in order to lose control of your mind and body, you are opening a door. That is why the Bible tells you not to be drunk with wine. Do not give your body over to a substance where you lose control. Continually opening this door could cause you to eventually become addicted to that substance physically and spiritually.

Generational Curses

God is a God of generations. He is the God of Abraham, Isaac, and Jacob. God designed the generations to be a highway of blessings that flow from one generation to another. The people of Israel entered the Promised Land to inhabit cities they did not build, eat from vineyards they did not plant, and drink from wells they did not dig. This land was promised to Abraham and his descendants. The blessing flowed to this horde of Israelites who came from Egypt who were only qualified because they were descendants of Abraham. God remembers His covenant for a thousand generations (Ps. 105:8).

This generational highway of blessing can also be a highway of cursing because both can travel down generational lines. Even though it doesn't seem right (Ezek. 18), there is a loophole that the enemy exploits. In the midst of the ten commandments that prohibit worshiping any other God, Exodus 20:5 says, *"You shall not worship them or serve them; for I, the Lord your God, am a jealous God, visiting the iniquity of the fathers on the children, on the third and the fourth generations of those who hate Me"* (also Num. 14:18).

A familiar spirit is a spirit that travels down family lines. It attaches to a covenant or agreement made in a previous generation. These could be things like a word curse, a vow, a sinful lifestyle, or a pact with the devil. Many of these ancestral choices may have been unintentional, but any ongoing agreement with sin will ultimately establish a spiritual contract, which results in bondage. Others are intentional, they simply don't realize how their vows affect future generations. Masonic vows fall into that category.[1] Generational curses are one reason we find demons in children who are not actively doing anything to open a door.

Whenever you can't find an open door in the seeker's personal story, no choices that account for the presence of a demonic spirit, look up his ancestral line. I had a spirit of rage all my life until I was set free in my mid-twenties. It was in my family line. Some hereditary diseases, conditions, and weaknesses can be caused by familiar spirits.

The good news is that in Christ you have a covenant sealed with His blood that overrides any ancestral covenant. You can ask God to examine any covenants or agreements that have been made on your behalf, and, if they are not righteous and just, you can ask Him to annul them. You might think this should be automatic, but not necessarily. Some of the benefits you are entitled to as a child of God must be intentionally claimed and your rights enforced.

Curses

There is power in the words you speak. James 3:1-12 spells out the power of the tongue. The tongue sets the course of a person's life like the bit in the horse's mouth or the rudder of a ship. It has the power to set a whole forest on fire. The tongue is the key to controlling the whole body and will set the course of one's life into blessing or into destruction.

Words have substance and assignments. They have the power to accomplish what you send them to do. Proverbs 18:21 says that death and life are in the power of the tongue. Whatever you come into agreement with is what you empower. Because the devil has been stripped of all authority and publicly humiliated (Col. 2:14-15), his only recourse is to deceive you into agreeing with his lies. Agreement empowers lies and releases the assignments of those words to bear fruit.

If a parent tells a child he is stupid, the child's agreement with those words releases their assignment and the child becomes stupid. Hopefully, the child will grow into an adult who receives the truth and is able to take back lost ground. Words spoken over you by others carry an assignment either for blessing or cursing and your agreement will either empower angels or empower demons.

Some curses sent against you, although not said to you directly, will still have an impact. My father agreed to pastor a large church in crises. During his short tenure there he brought things into order. That upset a lot of people and many left the church. He told me how the weight of the words spoken against him and his leadership team for the decisions they made strongly oppressed his leadership team. Their weekly practice of leadership prayer before Sunday services to break every ungodly assignment of words spoken against him, the leadership team, and the church finally shifted the atmosphere and removed the oppression.

Curses can be intentional, such as those spoken by people involved in witchcraft. They can also come from those ignorant of the power of words who verbalize their thoughts toward you, unaware they are listening to demons. Curses can also come from within yourself as you verbalize negative thoughts that may sound like you but are actually demonic in origin. These are inner vows and become self-inflicted wounds. If you have thoughts that ring of self-condemnation and self-judgment, those aren't yours even though you might have entertained them long enough that they sound like they are yours.

Curses can be the harvest you reap from the words that have gone out from you. Luke 6:28 says, *"Bless those who curse you, pray for those who mistreat you."* You might not feel like blessing your enemies, but there is a great reason to do so. Later in that chapter in verses 35-37 it says:

> *But love your enemies, and do good, and lend, expect-*
> *ing nothing in return; and your reward will be great,*
> *and you will be sons of the Most High; for He Himself*
> *is kind to ungrateful and evil men. Be merciful, just as*

*your Father is merciful. Do not judge, and you will not
be judged; and do not condemn, and you will not be
condemned; pardon, and you will be pardoned.*

The reason you need to do this is found in the next verse: "*Give,
and it will be given to you. They will pour into your lap a good measure—pressed down, shaken together, and running over. For by your
standard of measure it will be measured to you in return*" (Luke
6:38).

What comes out of you returns in a greater measure than what
you sent out. If blessing is going out of your mouth, those words
have an assignment and you reap a harvest of blessing. If negative
words, judgment, complaining, condemnation, and such are coming
out of you, then you are reaping a harvest of cursing. If a person feels
like people are always judging him, he might want to check what he
has been speaking. There is a reason why the apostle Paul said, "*Let
no unwholesome word proceed from your mouth, but only such a word
as is good for edification according to the need of the moment, so that it
will give grace to those who hear*" (Eph. 4:29).

The good news is that you can break the power of any word
that is not from heaven off of you. Galatians 3:13 says that Jesus
became a curse for you and redeemed you from the curse of the law.
Having become a curse for you means that it is your birthright to
be free from any curse. You can enforce what was gained on your
behalf through the cross of Christ and break every assignment of
hell against you.

Trauma

Trauma leaves people emotionally weakened. When someone is
in that vulnerable state, our adversary, who doesn't play fair, will

attempt to take advantage. Trauma can include long-term illness, automobile accidents, rape, physical abuse, violence, and war. Those who work with trauma victims, including first responders and the medical community, can also experience trauma as they attend to these victims. One reason we pray for people who are experiencing trauma is to give them a hedge of protection so that the adversary is unable to take advantage of them.

The best material I have seen on addressing trauma comes from Dr. Mike Hutchings. His material on "Healing PTSD" is thorough and effective for breaking off trauma. Though his material isn't in written form at the time of this writing, you can access it through Global Awakening's online bookstore: https://globalawakeningstore.com (also www.godhealsptsd.com).

Involuntary Exposure to Evil

You cannot always control what you are exposed to. Sometimes the door to trauma is opened for you. You may see or experience things that subject you to fear or imprint images on your mind that the adversary later uses to torment you.

One father who attended my church in the early 1980s was preparing to be away from his family for a season because of naval deployment. He decided to spend some time with their four-year-old son watching a movie. Though he regretted it later, he picked the movie *Poltergeist*. During his deployment, his wife noticed the son would not sleep by himself and he wanted the light left on at night. Each night started with a crying fit. Later she said she noticed not only was something off during the evenings but, one time when she was driving and singing worship songs, her son asked her to quit singing about Jesus.

It all came to a head one night while he was throwing another crying fit before bed. He suddenly became silent, looked around, and said, "Mama, I can't see!" He had gone blind. That demon picked the wrong mama to mess with. It was only a matter of seconds before it left once her "mama bear button" got pushed.

By the way, when ministering to young children parents can address any demonic presence while the child is asleep. Parents have authority over their children and authority over anything that is attached to their children. If the spirit doesn't leave, ask the Holy Spirit to reveal what doors need to be closed. This works for young children. If the child is old enough to cooperate with the spirit, the child must be included in the prayers so he can participate in obtaining his own freedom.

Grandparents often ask if they can exercise authority over their grandchildren. However, parents have primary authority over their children unless the grandparents are functioning as heads of that household. What grandparents can do is teach their grandchildren to fight spiritual battles. Children don't have a junior Holy Spirit.

Unforgiveness

Unforgiveness is a major open door to the demonic. Jesus addressed the issue of unforgiveness many times to emphasize the scriptural necessity to forgive others. Once you have freely received God's forgiveness, you give up any right to hold on to any offense against others. God gives you the grace to forgive. When you refuse to freely give what you were freely given, you step away from God's protection. Many spirits of infirmity have come through the open door of unforgiveness and bitterness. I have seen more people healed and set free from the simple act of forgiving somebody than any other activity.

If you truly understood forgiveness, what it is and what it isn't, you would have no problem forgiving another. Forgiveness isn't saying that what that person did is now OK or that you have somehow come to terms with it. Forgiveness isn't excusing it or forgetting it. Rather, forgiveness is an act that removes the power from that event. Forgiveness isn't being reconciled to the person. Reconciliation requires two people and you have no control over the other person. Whatever that person does or does not do, you are still required to forgive. Forgiveness isn't releasing any emotional boundaries that you may have established to prevent you from further emotional wounding. Forgiveness is giving up what you are owed by the offender and it actually releases you to go on with life untethered to the actions of others. Forgiving another benefits you more than the person you are forgiving. One of the reasons I wrote my book *Forgiveness* was to help people who are struggling to release past offenses wrestle through the issue and obtain freedom.

Wounding of the Heart

The cross of Christ is big enough to defeat every work of the enemy intended to destroy a person's life. Every hurt and wound designed to emotionally cripple and prevent the fulfillment of God's destiny has already been bought and paid for by Jesus on the cross. The cross of Christ can bring complete healing and wholeness to any emotional wound if a person is willing to take that wounding to the foot of the cross and leave it there. The issue isn't whether there is complete healing and wholeness provided by the cross of Christ. The issue revolves around one's readiness to take everything to the cross to receive the healing that already belongs to him.

While everything is fully accomplished by the cross of Christ, appropriating that provision may be a process. It is a process of letting Jesus have access to everything in your past, seeing it through His eyes, and embracing His truth so that you can put it behind you and move forward. Cutting off the old and putting on the new is part of the process of moving into maturity. You do not have permission to look at your past except through the eyes of Jesus, which are full of mercy and grace, free from condemnation and shame.

The demonic seek to hide in areas that are kept in the dark. When you protect darkness because of condemnation and shame, an unclean spirit may be driving those feelings. Bringing those areas into the light initiates healing and freedom. There can be a strong relationship between inner healing and deliverance because healing the heart shuts doors to the demonic.

Rebellion

In Matthew 8:5-13, Jesus encountered a centurion who wanted Him to pray for his servant to be healed. When Jesus offered to go to his house the centurion said it wasn't necessary because he understood authority. The centurion said, *"Lord, I am not worthy for You to come under my roof, but just say the word, and my servant will be healed. For I also am a man under authority, with soldiers under me; and I say to this one, 'Go!' and he goes, and to another, 'Come!' and he comes, and to my slave, 'Do this!' and he does it"* (Matt. 8:8-9). He believed that Jesus could speak the word and the servant would be healed. The centurion understood that because he was under authority, he was able to exercise authority. Those under him obeyed because he had delegated authority from those over him. His submission to authority meant that he could exercise authority.

In the same way, your submission to God and His delegated authorities empowers you to exercise His authority. Your rebellion against God and His delegated authorities removes you from the delegated flow of God's authority and you are on your own. This is the demonic strategy to strip God's authority from you in order to gain access to your life. Stepping out from under authority leaves a person vulnerable to the adversary's attacks and powerless to stop them. Submission is your only protection. Rebellion leaves you defenseless.

This is why believers are told to submit to God's delegated authorities and pray for them (Rom. 13:1-7; 1 Tim. 2:1-2; 1 Pet. 2:13-17; Heb. 13:7; Eph. 6:1-3; 1 Pet. 2:18-23). Submission is an issue of honor. Honor doesn't always mean agreement. You submit to the delegated authority as long as it doesn't violate God's laws because God's laws have absolute authority (Acts 4:19-20). Rebellion is a heart issue. If you are rebellious in your heart, you are vulnerable.

Religion

This next open door may surprise you if you define "religious" as being devoted in your behavior, activities, and commitment to God. However, what I'm addressing is not about being committed to God but rather being committed to traditions and ways of worship more than your devotion to pursue God. This is what Jesus regularly addressed with the Pharisees who were religious to a fault. They were upset when Jesus healed on the Sabbath (Matt. 12:10; Mark 3:2). Some of Jesus' harshest words were directed at the Pharisees in their religious hypocrisy. In Mark 7:8-9, Jesus says, *"'Neglecting the commandment of God, you hold to the tradition of men.' He was also saying to them, 'You are experts at setting aside the commandment of God in order to keep your tradition.'"* The religious leaders of Jesus' day were so consumed with tradition that they missed God. Jesus said in John 5:39-40, *"You search the Scriptures because you think that in them you have eternal life; it is these that testify about Me; and you are unwilling to come to Me so that you may have life."* They could not see God who was standing right in front of them because they were blinded by their devotion to tradition.

A religious spirit will fight against the Holy Spirit to protect the traditions of man. The devil is quite content for people to be consumed by religious activities, even activities done in the name of God, as long as they don't pursue God Himself.

ENDNOTE

1. A very concise yet thorough description of the effects of Freemasonry can be found in Randy Clark's book, *The Biblical Guidebook to Deliverance,* (Charisma House, 2015), 110-137. Also included in that chapter is a very thorough prayer to break off any effects of spoken curses that would want to travel down generational lines.

Chapter 5

──────────────────────

PROTOCOLS AND CAUTIONS WHEN STARTING THE MINISTRY SESSION

IT WAS THE SUMMER OF 1982, EIGHT MONTHS AFTER MY OWN personal freedom, when I ministered to my first demonized person. We had moved to Washington State for my first senior pastor position, when we took this first step down a road I never thought I would travel. By that time I had told my wife about my experience and we were both doing whatever reading on the topic I could find, which wasn't much in 1982.

One day my wife came home from a luncheon appointment to tell me about her visit with a young lady in our church. If you knew this lady you would not suspect she had any big issues. She was faithful in her attendance, loved the Lord, and had a sweet demeanor. Underneath that, however, fear dominated her to such an extent that she organized her life around it. Mentally she knew that there was no basis for that fear so she sought counsel from my wife.

My wife asked her if she thought it might be demonic.

She responded, "You think it might be?"

My wife then said, "I don't know. Why don't you come over to the house tonight and let Rodney minister to you?"

When she repeated that conversation I went into panic mode. "I can't believe you told her she could come over! I don't know what I'm doing! I've never done this before! Why did you tell her to come over?"

Then she reminded me that, after all, I was her pastor and who else is supposed to do that? She had a point. She pulled out the *pastor card* and I knew I had no choice.

I immediately called my dad, who was pastoring a large Baptist church in Tulsa, Oklahoma. "Dad, I need your help. A woman is coming over tonight who I think is demonized and I need to know what to do. Have any ideas?"

He answered, "Don't ask me, I've never done it either. However, we have had a guest speaker this week. His name is Jim Hylton and he has been casting demons out of people all week long. He's here right now and I'll put him on."

I can recognize a divine appointment when I see one.

Jim was pastoring at that time in the Fort Worth area. As he took the phone I was ready for his download of wisdom on how to deal with demons. I grabbed my tape recorder and stuck it to my earpiece to record the conversation. I didn't take notes because, after all, I had a recording. Except, when I went to play it back later, it was completely blank. I wrote down everything I could recall, which was just a small portion of what he had said. Between that time and the moment she came over, I was deep in prayer!

She arrived right on time and we all sat down. I was really nervous because I had never done this before. I had never seen a deliverance (besides the one in *The Exorcist*), and didn't know how to begin. After some small talk I decided to read some scripture that I knew would irritate the demons in hopes of provoking them to do something. After I read the scriptures she smiled pleasantly and said, "Those are nice."

Nothing was happening.

I decided to pray. We all bowed our heads and closed our eyes—by the way, do *not* close your eyes when ministering in this area! I didn't know. No one told me the rules so all heads were bowed and eyes were closed. When I finished the prayer my wife and I looked up at each other but the lady couldn't open her eyes. She started to panic and said, "I can't open my eyes!"

I responded, "What do you mean you can't open your eyes?"

"Just what I said, I am unable to open my eyes!"

At that moment I looked over to my wife and gave her "the look." The look that said, "What did you get us into!" I turned to the woman and said, "In the name of Jesus, I command those eyes to open!" Immediately her eyes popped open and I thought to myself, "Oh my, it worked!"

I sincerely wished we had never set this appointment, but, at that point, we were committed. Once you start you can't just quit. It's like when a pregnant woman feels those labor pains. She can't just decide to have the baby the following week because it would be more convenient. Once the demon started manifesting we were committed to finishing the process.

I started to talk and she got a very confused look on her face and said, "This isn't funny! I see your lips moving but I can't hear anything!" She had gone deaf.

I briefly glanced over to my wife and gave her "the look" again before turning back to the woman and saying, "In the name of Jesus, I command you to release her ears!" Immediately she could hear.

For the next several hours we ministered to her. It was one of the worst experiences of my life. If the demons could smell fear, they had no problem smelling it on me because I reeked of it. I really didn't know what I was doing but eventually they left. I don't know if they left because I cast them out or just wore them out, but they all left. I was drained and suffering from adrenaline overload. However, at the end of the night I saw the look of freedom on her face and knew it had all been worth it. I didn't like the mess of getting them out, but I loved the result. That's when I told the Lord that I was willing to endure the mess to see the look of freedom on someone's face. The very next week she still had that look and that gave me such joy!

Discerning There Actually Is a Demon

The act of deliverance should be an act of love where the person encounters the Lord Jesus who sets them free. As a representative of the Lord, you minister as He would with love, honor, and dignity. You make the person the priority. Ministry should not be centered around the demon but focused on the person and his freedom. There is a big difference.

You must first determine that you are actually dealing with a demon, so you need some discernment of the Holy Spirit. It can get confusing at times. Some manifestations of the demonic are similar to the manifestations of the Holy Spirit. In fact, the demonic try to imitate the Holy Spirit. At times you may be dealing with a person's wounds and not a demon. You might be dealing with his flesh. Using your discernment will determine your next step.

First Corinthians 12:10 talks about the gift of discerning or distinguishing of spirits. This spiritual gift discerns which spirit is operating in a person—a demonic spirit, the Holy Spirit, or the spirit of the person. This gift is a manifestational gift. That means that the Holy Spirit can drop one of these gifts on you at His choosing when He thinks you need it. God also gives it to you when you think you need it, if you will ask. You have not because you ask not (James 4:2).

Some people see into the spiritual realm and can see demons like others can see angels. I can't. I have seen them do things and I can sense them but I have never seen one and really don't care to. However, if you see demons and you don't see angels, something might be broken. If you can see into that realm, you should be able to see both. If not, just start looking for angels and you might start seeing them.

For me, one way that I sense the presence of demons is through what I call my *caution flag.* I have a common feeling when I get around them. It is a feeling of taking flight and running away. It is a feeling that I just want to move to Poteau, Oklahoma and work in the feed and seed store. I know that the demon is projecting that feeling on me. So, when I feel that particular feeling, I have learned to recognize that I'm dealing with an unclean spirit.

Demons will often project their assignment. This requires you to pay attention to what you are feeling when you are ministering to people. If I get next to a person and feel like behaving a particular way toward that person that is not the normal way I treat people, I take notice. For example, if I am looking at a couple of guys I've just met and both seem to be equal in about every way, but the guy on the right, I don't know why, I just don't like him. Why do I feel like that for the guy on the right and not the guy on the left? It could be that there is a spirit of rejection present and that spirit is projecting that so I will reject him.

If I were looking at a couple of women who were outwardly equal in age, beauty, and modestly dressed, but I found myself lusting and thinking inappropriate things about the woman on the right, but not the one on the left, I could be feeling what that spirit is projecting. Demons project their assignment and you can feel what they are projecting. This is why a person with a victim spirit and a person with an abusing spirit can find each other in a room full of people.

You have to know yourself and the way you interact with others in order to discern accurately. If it is your tendency to reject most people, you can't trust your discernment in that area. If you have a tendency to lust after most women, you can't trust your discernment in that area. You need to know your personal tendencies. If you feel like reacting to a person in a particular way that isn't appropriate, pay attention to that. Sit back and ask yourself if this is something rising out of you or is this something projecting from the person.

One thing you *don't* do is announce it. You don't say to that person, "My goodness, I see a spirit of rejection all over you!" You might be wrong. You don't want to put something on him that isn't there. Don't create a mess you have to clean up later. The way you handle this is to ask questions and help him discover if there are any demonic patterns or wounded areas that need to be healed. Let him discover what he has.

How About Mentally Ill People?

Some authors who have written books on deliverance have wrongly ascribed every mentally ill condition to the demonic. They fail to realize that the brain is an organ and can malfunction like a liver, a heart, colon, etc. The malfunction of the brain/mind may be a physical issue, a spiritual issue, or both. It might be caused by a demon or have a demon present, but you can't assume that every brain or mental dysfunction is demonic at the root. If it is, then deliverance should bring the person into normalcy. If it isn't, what he needs first is a physical healing of the brain. You will find demons present with many mentally ill people because demons like to take advantage of weakness and vulnerability. Just because you find demons there doesn't mean the source of the issue is demonic. You need to listen to the Holy Spirit. You don't want to abuse people who have mental issues if the source of the issue is biological or chemical.

Some friends of mine called me one day to come to their house because their 21-year-old daughter had flipped out. She was later diagnosed as being bipolar. For hours they rebuked demons with no success. When I got there I asked what they were doing and they told me how they were casting everything out. I asked if it was working.

They said, "No, that's why we called you."

I suggested that might not be the right approach in this case. Even though there might have been some demonic involvement, there were other issues involved.

Some people exhibit dissociative patterns. Often these are people who have gone through some sort of abuse very early in life. If a person went through abuse when very young, he may have developed patterns of dissociation where his brain went into survival mode and partitioned. This means some parts of the brain dissociated, or separated, from other parts. It was a protective pattern that enabled him to survive as a child but becomes dysfunctional if it still remains in an adult. If this happens, the individual will end up going through life with a fragmented mind, fragmented personalities, and fragmented memories.

The brain is very wonderfully made. The body is designed to survive. However, these dissociated parts aren't demons. There may be demons attached to some parts and there may be some demons masquerading as other parts, but the healing of that person won't happen through casting out a bunch of demons. It will require healing the wounds each personality carries. The mind might be fragmented but the spirit is not. Bring all those personalities to the Holy Spirit who resides in his spirit.

Physical Manifestations

One obvious way to discern the presence of a demon is when it manifests in a person's body. Not all manifestations are demonic. It could be the person or his flesh reacting to the manifest presence of the Holy Spirit. Therefore, when you see a manifestation of some sort, even though it doesn't always mean there is a demonic spirit, it is enough to check it out. Remember that when a demon manifests, it isn't a first choice. They prefer to live in darkness in stealth mode, not out in the open. Manifestations are often the demon's tactic to get you to quit. It should be an encouragement to you because often it is a sign their time is up with that person.

Manifestations are sometimes the demon's way to humiliate someone. If a person starts tearing off his clothes, doing body movements that are vulgar, or similar acts, the spirit wants to shame him. Your job is to protect the person's dignity. You have authority to rebuke the manifestation, take authority, and stop that manifestation.

Following are some common manifestations. This certainly isn't an exhaustive list because there can be more dramatic manifestations depending on how deeply the person was embedded in the demonic realm.

If pain moves around in the body, that is a spirit of infirmity. If you are praying for a person's shoulder and the pain moves from the shoulder to the leg, that is certainly a spirit. Spirits of infirmity may be tied to an open door that needs to be closed but often they are loosely attached and go quickly.

If a person goes into a sudden drowsiness or even a drunken stupor as if he just took a lot of valium, that is very suspicious. Those demons intend to put him to sleep to prevent his cooperating in the deliverance.

Facial contortions stretch the face in abnormal ways. It's not always a sure sign of a demon as the flesh can also react with grimaces and other intense expressions, but when I see it I'm suspicious.

Screaming was a common demonic reaction to Jesus (Mark 1:26; Luke 4:33). You may also hear screaming if a wound of the heart comes to the surface and the person reacts to the pain. That may not be demonic at all. However, if there is screaming, you need to check out the source.

I am really suspicious if a person's body becomes rigid or frozen. That could be angels restraining him to stop the spirits from doing something through his body. I was in the "deliverance tent" at a crusade in Brazil one time. The deliverance tent is where they took the people who manifested so violently that the ministry team needed more help. I was brought to a man who was involved in Macumba, a common form of Brazilian witchcraft. He was a brand-new believer who needed to get cleaned up. They sat him down in a chair and when my team came to get him, he growled at us. Growling is a good sign you are dealing with a demon.

We tried to get him to walk to the area where we were ministering but he was frozen in the sitting position. He could not unbend his body. Ever resourceful, we just picked up the chair with him in it. Now, I'm always suspicious when a body is rigid. However, when you read about some of the early revivals, you will see that some people became stiff for hours or days while working through repentance issues. Until I experience the intensity of that sort of spiritual revival, I will probably continue to be suspicious.

Lack of eye contact is a sure bet there is a demon present. I'm not talking about the wounded person who just can't make eye contact in normal life. If you ask the person to look into your eyes and he can't because his eyes are looking all over the place or rolling back in his head, that is a pretty good indication a spirit is present. The eyes are a great place of discernment. There is something about the eyes that look into the soul. There is also a glazed-over look that will appear in the eyes that indicates a spirit is present. I really don't know how to accurately describe what this looks like, but once you see it you will never forget it. I can be talking to a person and can discern that the conversation has just crossed over to talking to the demon. The person doesn't realize that he is not in control of his own thoughts.

If someone's voice changes, if he speaks with a voice that does not sound like him, that indicates the presence of an evil spirit. A spirit is able to constrict the vocal chords to produce a higher pitch or loosen them to go lower. The person's own vocal chords are contorted to sound like a different voice. Rarely does a voice actually belong to a different entity, but it has happened.

Some notice a foul sulfuric smell while ministering to a demonized person. Because not everybody smells it, we assume this represents some kind of supernatural discernment. I have had a whole team ministering where only some smelled anything. This is not a discerning gift that I would actually ask for but God gave it to me anyway.

The list could go on and on. It isn't my intention to describe every manifestation that's been seen but simply to make you are aware of what you might encounter. How much the person has interacted with demons will determine the severity of the manifestations, from subtle voice changes, to emulating animals and reptiles, to levitating. Don't be afraid, just know who you are in Jesus and what arsenal you possess. If you are in Jesus you possess a huge arsenal!

Ask Probing Questions

Identifying demonic influence isn't always based on what is obvious or what is sensed. Sometimes you can just ask questions. Ask if he hears voices. I'm not referring to the voice of the Holy Spirit. Is he hearing voices as if someone is talking to him? Has he interacted with a spirit guide? Has he communicated with the dead? Even if he thinks he is hearing God, ask him about the content of the message. If a voice says to live with the boyfriend or girlfriend and fornicate, you know that wasn't God. I was a prayer counselor in a prayer tent for a Christian concert when a man told me how God gave him new scripture. It didn't take me long to figure out that he was listening to the wrong channel.

Ask if there is uncontrollable sin. If he knows he is going to do it even though he doesn't really want to, but finds himself doing it anyway followed by great remorse, an evil spirit is driving that.

Ask about uncontrollable behavior. It may not be an area of sin, just a behavior and compulsion that is out of control. It may have started out as a habit and turned into a compulsion. Those aren't always demonic, but it bears checking out.

Is he ruled by abnormal emotions? Some emotions are normal based on the stimuli. If a woman is walking to her car in a dark parking lot, apprehension and anxiety could be pretty normal. If she is consumed with anxiety walking out to her car in her driveway in a relatively crime-free neighborhood in the middle of the day, the circumstances don't warrant the intensity of those emotions. If a person experiences an overwhelming emotion that the circumstances don't warrant, examine more deeply. It could be a dominating fear that you recognize as unrealistic but feels real to him. If a person is out of control with areas like rejection, bitterness, rage, anxiety, self-hatred, and depression, emotions that are ruling and destroying his life, there could be an evil spirit behind it. A person going down the road of severe depression to the point of suicide has entertained self-destructive thoughts fed to him by the demonic.

Believers versus Unbelievers

The question of whether or not deliverance should be done with an unbeliever is an important one to work through. When you look at the gospels and the book of Acts it seems that every deliverance involved an unbeliever. What you need to take into consideration is what Jesus said in Matthew 12:43-45: if the house is left empty the demons can return to the person and bring seven worse.

One time when I was in India training pastors, we did an outreach in a local pastor's village. We arrived as they were leaving the fields and making their way home for the evening. A group from the church sang their songs loudly and attracted the crowd. I preached the gospel and then we prayed for the sick. As we were ministering, one of the team members tapped me on the shoulder and told me that Pastor Peter, one of the pastors we were training, needed some help. I looked over and Pastor Peter was standing over a woman sitting on the ground and manifesting demonically. He had a handful of her hair and looked like he was trying to shake the demons out.

I grabbed my interpreter and quickly intervened, for which I'm sure the woman was very thankful. I asked her if she wanted to receive Christ. She initially wanted to receive Jesus until she found out that she would have to renounce all her other gods that had been in her family for generations. She decided she couldn't do that. We talked to her a little more, prayed for her, blessed her, and she went on her way. The next day in the training session we discussed the event (without embarrassing Pastor Peter for his hair-yanking techniques). We could have eventually gotten demons out of her but her unwillingness to give her whole life to Christ meant that she would have just gone home and invited them back in plus, potentially, a whole lot more.

In this situation I follow a guideline not a rule. The way I explain it is, a rule is something that you always follow regardless of the situation. You don't break the rules. For example, if you are married, you stay faithful. That's a rule. A guideline is something you follow but can be broken if the Holy Spirit leads. My guideline is that I don't do deliverance on unbelievers because they don't have the Holy Spirit to fill them up. However, some people need to be delivered first so they can make a decision to choose Christ. You must listen to the Holy Spirit. If I don't hear anything from the Holy Spirit, then I follow the guideline and don't minister deliverance. However, if the Holy Spirit says to go ahead and do deliverance on this unbeliever, I obey the Holy Spirit. I often get permission from the Holy Spirit to remove spirits of infirmity from unbelievers so God can get their attention in order to extend an invitation to know Him.

Chapter 6

HELPING PEOPLE PARTICIPATE, NOT SPECTATE

ONCE A PERSON ENTERS A RELATIONSHIP WITH JESUS, HE needs to know his true identity in Christ and the new authority he now carries. He needs to know that he overwhelmingly conquers all things through Jesus (Rom. 8:37). The best way for him to comprehend this belief system is to actively participate in ridding himself of any unwanted spirit rather than passively letting someone else do it for him.

If you are teaching a child to eat with a spoon, you put a spoon in his hand and walk him through the motions of feeding himself. If you don't teach him to feed himself, he will be dependent on someone else forever. Growing up in the faith will require the immature to begin to take personal responsibility for walking out his salvation.

Deal with the Person, Not the Spirit

Most of the people I minister to have no demonic manifestations at all. The few times they begin to manifest, I call the name of the person until I know that I'm talking to him and not to a demon. I encourage him with the truth that he has authority over his own body and authority over the demon that is attempting to manifest. I then encourage him to take authority over that spirit and over his body.

One of my spiritual sons made an appointment for a man to whom others had tried to minister. The man could not get through a session without going into strong demonic manifestation. My spiritual son hadn't seen any strong manifestations and was hoping this would be his chance. As we ministered to this man I could tell that there had been some great advancement in his healing with major things already broken off of his life. I sensed an impending manifestation about the same time that he said he felt he was about to manifest.

I asked him, "Why do you let them to that to you?"

"Do what?" he responded.

"Manifest. Don't you know you have authority over your body and authority over that demon? You don't have to let them do that to you."

"Really?" he questioned.

"Really!" I affirmed.

Once I encouraged him in his true identity in Christ and the authority he had as a son of God, he didn't manifest at all. It was the first time he exercised that authority, because in all of his previous sessions no one ever told him about his true identity. My spiritual son was a little disappointed in not seeing a demonic manifestation, but in lieu of that, he did acknowledge that the man walked away empowered.

On rare occasions someone may go unconscious as the demons take over or are manifesting in such a way that you know you are not talking to the person. When that happens I begin to call the name of the person until he is conscious and aware. My objective is to help him exercise the authority he has in Christ. People don't know they have the power to say "no" to demons because they have believed the lie that they have no control. By default, because of this ignorance, they yield total control to an ungodly entity. If I only speak to the demon and not the person, then I am exercising *my* authority but I am not taking advantage of the authority that lies in the afflicted person to expedite the freedom process. Pulling him in as a participant releases that authority. Rebuke the spirit and call the person forward as you encourage him with the victory he can have.

I was on a ministry team in a church in Brazil when I was called over to minister to a young woman in full demonic manifestation, writhing on the floor surrounded by people yelling at the demon. I took my good translator to find out her name. I recognized her as one who had responded to the call for salvation so she was a new believer who simply needed some cleaning up. Once I knew her name was Anna, I knelt down and began to call her by name until I could see the look in her eye and the expression on her face and knew it was her and not a demon. I explained that, as a follower of Christ, she now has authority over that spirit and doesn't have to let that spirit humiliate her anymore. I felt the Lord had shown me the open door, and when we started addressing it she went back into the demonic manifestation again. So I was pretty sure we were on the right track. The problem was that I had to start again, calling her name over and over until I got her back. We addressed the issue and closed the door and she was set free.

Calling the person forward to participate works most of the time. I have to say "most of the time" because there are rare situations when it doesn't seem to work. I was in a township near Johannesburg, South Africa, ministering after the message and began to pray for a woman who had come out of witchcraft. Her whole family were witch doctors and she was the first Christian. As I started to pray for her she fell to the floor in full demonic manifestation. Nothing I did brought her to awareness. I had to leave her on the floor.

When a person isn't consciously present, you must step back and give him some time. They will eventually recover, which she did and went home. The next day as soon as the first song started she fell over again into a demonic manifestation. I never did get to really talk to her that first year but did so when I returned a year later. Because of her experience in witchcraft, she had given herself over to those demons so many times that she didn't know how to exercise authority over them. Her agreement with the demons' lies that she was powerless to do anything actually empowered them. To that church's credit, they worked with her throughout the year to address her wounded soul. They spoke into her true identity in Christ to give her confidence and courage to take her rightful authority.

Invoke the Person's Will to Participate

I will often ask the seeker (the person seeking deliverance) if he wants to be free. On occasion I will ask him if he wants to get rid of that spirit or if he wants to keep it. I know that sounds like an absurd question, but I have had some who have chosen to keep the demons. When I was first doing deliverance, I bypassed people's will and just focused on getting the demon out. It never occurred to me to ask the seeker if he wanted it gone. On one occasion, after the demon left, a woman said with a tone of regret, "I'm going to miss that one." I about went through the roof! I couldn't believe that someone would want to keep anything like that. Then the Lord reminded me how I had personally become friends with one of my demons because of what it did for me. Now I ask because I want that person's will to be fully involved.

There is power in a person's will. There is power in agreement. Oftentimes that demon is present because the person came into agreement with something. This agreement empowers the demon. The solution requires the person to agree with God's will to remove the spirit. If a stronghold exists in that person's mind and is dominating his will, you must unravel the lies he has agreed to. You need him to participate, not just cooperate. There is greater success when the person is choosing to be free rather than you doing it for him. That is why I ask if he wants to be free. Most of the time he will say "yes." However, I must recognize that what he says and what he means may not be the same.

Involving the person's will was one of the huge shifts in how I did deliverance. When I first started doing deliverance, I did not have any mentors to follow. I ministered primarily through power encounters. I confronted the demons and took them on in my own authority. I treated the seeker as a spectator, merely observing and cooperating, while I did all the work. Sometimes these sessions lasted for hours because I was trying to get every demon out, whether the seeker wanted them out or not.

The shift came after an encounter with one of my church leaders in a staff meeting. I noticed that Sally (not her real name), our Sunday school director, was clenching her teeth and her fisted hand shook like she had tremors. When I asked if she was OK she explained, through clenched teeth, that she didn't know why but she

93

wanted to hit me in the face except that her fist was frozen. It didn't take a rocket scientist to figure out there was a demon involved. That was mid-morning and we finished ministering to her around dinner time. She came back the next day for another seven to eight hours and then the third day for three to four more hours.

One of the problems of these long sessions is they will burn out the team. Long sessions consume your time, your strength, and your will to fight. Demons strategize to siphon off your strength. If you want to burn out a team, do the power encounters exclusively. Power encounters are unavoidable at times. Jesus did a lot of them, because when you bring the Kingdom of God into a new place it will always clash with the kingdom of darkness. However, when it comes to cleaning up the sheep, there is a more effective and permanent approach.

Without going into a lot of detail, it is enough to say that Sally had come from a difficult background. There had also been some witchcraft in her family. One of her close aunts held séances and similar things. Sally inherited a lot of her possessions because her aunt didn't have children of her own. There was a lot to be broken off and I was determined to get rid of every demon that we could find. At the end of the third day she walked out feeling very free.

A couple of weeks later she called to report she had another one. It's not uncommon, after you go through the outer layer, for the Lord to give a person a breather to assimilate the new level of freedom before going deeper. Sally had rested briefly, but it was time to go a little deeper and another demon had popped up. She called in a panic but I assured her that I could help take care of it. At this point in my ministry, because of my success rate, I had some arrogance. OK, maybe a lot of arrogance—which isn't a good idea when you minister in this area (James 4:6-7). I sort of knew how those disciples felt when the demons were subject to them and they walked around with their chests puffed out, proud that demons submitted to them (Luke 10). At the time I wasn't taking Jesus' advice to resist pride and rejoice that my name was written in heaven (Luke 10:20).

Sally came on over to the church and we started ministering to her. Nothing worked. I pulled everything out of my tool belt and could not budge that demon. Then I decided to ask the Holy Spirit what was going on. Asking the Holy Spirit should have been the first thing that I did, not just my last resort because nothing else was working. However, I knew my authority and knew that demons submitted to it and that had worked just fine in the past. This is where the Lord was trying to teach me that it wasn't my ministry but His. I was co-ministering with Him and needed to be listening to His instructions, not riding off of my past successes.

When I inquired of the Holy Spirit, He spoke very clearly, "You are not fighting against this demon, you are fighting her will." That word was as clear as if it were audible.

I sat back and said, "The Lord just spoke to me very clearly. I'm not fighting a demon, I'm fighting against your will. You don't want this thing gone!"

"Oh yes I do! I want this thing gone and I need you to help me do it," she cried.

She pleaded with me to keep working but I knew what I'd heard. "No, I heard very clearly. I'm done. If you can't get that thing out, you are just going to have to learn to live with it."

She got that demon out in less than five minutes! This was a valuable lesson that forever changed how I did ministry. From then on, I included the person as a participant rather than a spectator. The free will God has given each of us must be engaged!

I learned some valuable lessons from that encounter. I learned that you don't have to get every demon out. People come in with demons and they can go home with them. After all, they have probably had those things for years. When I realized that God is more interested in a whole heart than the expulsion of demons, I could wait until their will was involved and they wanted to be free.

I learned that I can't be the go-to person when someone needs freedom. The Lord is! Some deliverance ministers are gratified that others are dependent on them. It feeds the ego and gives them purpose but it isn't healthy and it doesn't empower the seeker. You cannot allow people to become dependent on the team members to defeat the adversary. They must learn to fight for themselves. If you don't teach them to fight, you are encouraging them to depend on you rather than the Holy Spirit. If you don't teach them how to fight, then you will always be fighting their battles for them.

When I began to approach deliverance this way, my entire perspective changed. When I got those calls at 2 A.M. for help with a manifesting demon, I told them to take care of it and call me tomorrow and tell me how it came out. They had that demon in the middle of the afternoon and didn't call, why should I let a demon determine my agenda?

With the person fully engaged as a participant, I quit talking to demons and began talking to the person. Ministers often talk to demons to find inroads and open doors. That was my go-to process for the longest time. Even though demons lie and try to deceive, through experience you start to discern when they are trying to pull one over you. You can eventually figure things out. Then I began to realize I was modeling a behavior that said, basically, when you want to get information, just talk to a demon. Why would I want to talk to a demon when the Holy Spirit can give us the right information?

I wanted to model listening to the Holy Spirit so I quit talking to demons. I began to help the seeker hear God's voice and ask the Holy Spirit what he needed to know. Sometimes it took a while for him to recognize which voice was the Holy Spirit, but that's why we were there to help. You can sometimes get the information more quickly from the demonic rather than working with the person to discern the voice of God, but it is an inferior way to minister. Jesus only conversed with demons once. Personally, I think when Jesus was asking, "*What is your name?*" (Mark 5:9), He wasn't talking to the demons to get information. He was asking the person and the demons answered.

Are there exceptions, rare situations, when the believer cannot participate but you do the ministry anyway? Yes there are, depending on the amount of fragmentation and wounding. The extremely wounded soul may not, at least initially, be able to cooperate during ministry. You might have to do all the work in the beginning. However, you want him to begin to take responsibility and exercise authority as soon as possible.

Command the Demon to Do What You Want It to Do

I never presume that there is any legal right for a spirit to be in a Christian. The first thing I do is simply command the demon to go without looking for the legal right. It could be very loosely attached and there may be no need to go into why it is there. Sometimes I don't even tell the person a demon is involved. One lady came for prayer at the end of an evening worship service. As we prayed she said, "It feels like something wants to leave."

I responded, "Let's just tell it to leave!"

We did, she jerked a bit, gave a big cough, and then felt better. When she asked what that was I didn't feel led to explain the mechanics of demons leaving a person. I just said, "I guess God was cleaning something out of you." She was happy with that response and went her way.

When working with someone who knows he is dealing with a demon, I tell the seeker that the first thing we need to do is to command this unclean spirit to leave. Usually we do it together as I get him involved immediately in pursuing his freedom. If he struggles with what to say I can model it or have him repeat after me commanding it to go.

I don't typically tell departing spirits where to go when they leave a person. Jesus said in Matthew 12:43 that when the spirit leaves a person it goes to dry or waterless places, but I don't see any model in the New Testament where someone sent them there. I don't think you can send them to hell before their time. I guess you can tell them to go where Jesus sends them, but I'm wondering if they aren't already going there. There aren't any models in scripture that give us instructions on how to do that. Jesus gave them permission to go into a bunch of pigs one time but He didn't send them there. I do know that there are angels present that can escort them where Jesus wants them escorted. Some people fear the demons will jump to one of the team members. If that is your concern, then you can prohibit them from touching any team member, their families, or their spiritual community.

You don't have to know the demons' names to get them out. With some, it is helpful to know their assignment and that assignment will have a name like fear, suicide, hate, etc. If it were important to know the name, then that would have been repeatedly modeled in scripture. As I said earlier, the only time Jesus asked for a name was when, I believe, he was talking to the person and the demons responded. Oftentimes demons will respond to any name you give them. Remember, you are dealing with unclean spirits in the spiritual realm. Your communication is actually spirit to spirit even though you are voicing it verbally. That is why you can be in another country ministering to someone who doesn't speak or understand your language yet those demons respond to your words. You can pretty much use any name and get a reaction because you are communicating spirit to spirit. Knowing the unclean spirit's assignment is helpful, however, so you can close the doors that gave them access.

People don't have to throw up to get the demons out. If they feel sick at their stomach, command that spirit to release them from any nausea. It is so interesting to me to see how different cultures have different manifestations. In one they may throw up, in another they cough, and in another they burp. I'm not kidding you! If you have a certain expectation, demons seem to follow that protocol. The truth is, if you hand them a trash bag before the ministry session they will probably use it.

What If They Don't Leave When You Tell Them To?

If the demon doesn't leave after a moment or two, we have to investigate why it still remains. It could be that the legal right has not been thoroughly removed. The ground may not have been taken back as thoroughly as God would like. Apparently God won't deliver this person yet because that would leave the door open for something worse to come in. Sometimes I think God should remove something because it seems every legal right has been removed and yet it isn't happening. Then there are those times I am pretty sure that not all the legal rights have been removed and yet God delivers them. It's a mystery I can't explain.

God's primary objective is to heal the heart. He is thorough in doing that. Getting rid of demons is a fruit of that objective. Sometimes demons are like road signs. They point to the place of brokenness. "Broken heart—3 miles ahead," "Watch for fallen dreams," "Watch out: wounding ahead." God wants to heal the brokenness and bring restoration to the heart. Once God removes the demon's right and touches the heart, deliverance comes easily.

How Do You Know When They Are Gone?

This is a more subjective area because you must rely, at least somewhat, on the seeker rather than your own perceptions. He may feel lighter or may have actually felt it leave. His symptoms are gone. Sometimes he may experience a sense of "silence" or a void where something used to be. Many times he will experience peace. That does not mean everything has left, just whatever the Holy Spirit was dealing with at that time. Don't press the person for more deliverance if he is not ready or the Holy Spirit isn't prompting it.

For me, I can often feel when a spirit departs. I sense it and often I will feel the peace come over the person. If I don't feel the peace, then I will ask the Holy Spirit what He wants me to do. Often I will ask my team members what they are sensing. Unless there are some observable physical symptoms, this is a very subjective area.

One thing is for sure. If the seeker is done, then you are done. You rely on his participation, so if he is worn out or doesn't want to go any further, then his willful involvement is over as well and it is time to go home.

Chapter 7

WHAT ABOUT THOSE WHO ARE NOT SET FREE?

THERE ARE TIMES WHEN I FOLLOW ALL THE STEPS THAT I know and the spirit doesn't leave. The first thing to check is whether the seeker has closed all the doors he knows about. If that doesn't provide any answers there are a few other areas to examine.

Is There Any Intent to Fill Their Life Up with the Lord?

I will get into this in much more depth in the next few chapters, but here is the bottom line. Once a demon leaves its home, it may try to return. If that space is clean and empty, it invites seven worse into the old home and the latter state is worse for the seeker than the former one (Matt. 12:43-45). It is for your protection that you do not leave the house empty and unoccupied.

God is perfectly capable of removing any demon whether or not it has a legal right just because He's God. However, that person's long-term safety is more important to God than a short-term result. If the seeker wants to leave the door open, and may even plan on returning to it, God in His mercy may wait until he is willing to shut the door and keep it closed.

The Lord in His perfect knowledge knows your motivation. If you want that demon gone because it is an inconvenience but have no intention of filling your life with God's presence, He knows that. A stubborn demon might be God's mercy to keep you from going into a worse state. It is almost like God is saying, *"I don't want you to be in a worse condition, so until you are willing to go all the way with Me, this thing is here to drive you to that desperation."*

I was ministering to a man at the end of the Sunday service when it was apparent that a demon was popping up. I asked him if he wanted to keep it or get rid of it. To my surprise, he said that he'd like to keep it for now. I didn't argue with him and let him go his way. A few days later he phoned me, desperate, saying, "I'm ready to get rid of this thing now!" It is sort of like Jonah. A few days in the belly of a fish makes a person willing to go to Nineveh.

When the people of Israel were going to take the promised land, God said this to them, *"I will not do it all in one year, for the land would become a wilderness, and the wild animals would become too many to control. But I will drive them out a little at a time, until your population has increased enough to fill the land"* (Exod. 23:29-30 TLB).

God said that He would give them what they were able and willing to occupy. He would give them the land little by little. That is so the land would not become desolate and get out of control. The land was tame and usable, but if there was no one to take care of it, it would get out of control and be in a worse condition. Not only that, but God wanted to teach them to fight and take the land. If they fought to take it, they would know how to fight to hold it.

It's a great parallel for us. God will give you what you will occupy. It would be too much to occupy if you got completely free all at once. That could be overwhelming, so God may take His time as He trains you to occupy the ground you have reclaimed. If you have no intent to occupy that land, God is fully aware of that. Withholding total freedom (at this time) may be His mercy to prevent a worse condition.

There is no easy road to building godliness into your life. There is no quick fix without being an active participant and taking on the responsibility to rebuild a stronghold of righteousness to fill the void.

Displacement: Removing What Is Intertwined into Identity

Another situation where demons don't seem to leave is if the area of bondage is tied to the person's identity. In this case the demonic spirit isn't displaced because it clings to an embedded lie that the person still believes. The most difficult to remove demons that I have encountered were those the seeker permitted to remain, often unknowingly. They were so entrenched in the person's identity that it seemed that nothing I did, even with the person's participation, had any noticeable effect. I would tell it to go, the seeker would tell it to go, but it would not budge. I know the authority I carry, and I had schooled the person as much as I could, at least giving him head knowledge of his own authority. But whatever we did and said, it just wouldn't leave. In those cases we changed strategy from "casting out" to "displacement." It involved addressing the lies as well as the false identity the person embraced. When the truth hits the core of the person, light displaces darkness. Some spirits leave with inner healing, but on occasion I ran across someone who needed more because the lies were so entrenched.

If you have a fly in a cup, you can get it out one of two different ways. Use your fingers and pluck it out or put the cup under a faucet and flush it out. If you can't pluck it out, then you need to flush it out. Most of the time we just pluck demons out, but every once in a while we must employ a displacement strategy to flush out the darkness with light that is already in the believer.

I had been doing deliverance for several years when my wife and I were ministering to a woman who had a leadership position in her church. She was quite familiar with the inner-healing process and had gone through some (though she needed more inner healing). She came to the house for prayer and a demon manifested while my wife and I were ministering to her. Nothing we did could remove it. We tried on several subsequent occasions to cast it out before I just gave up. It was tied to her wounded heart. Others tried but it just didn't seem to work. She didn't like the demon but she did like the attention she was getting during ministry. She had a victim mentality, not an overcomer mentality, and thought like a victim. It had integrated into her identity to such an extent that it was how she saw herself. At that time, I had not thought through this kind of wounding so I didn't really know how to help her.

On another occasion I was ministering to a young woman who was a short-term missionary. She had gone through many different counseling and inner-healing sessions and received some relief but always found herself back in bondage soon after. She attributed her struggle to a time in her past when a person who was supposed to be her spiritual leader had hurt her and she was working through the hurt. In fact, she had worked through that same hurt many times. She also had a victim mentality. As I interviewed her I discovered that it was not just this time but it was a repetitious pattern in her life to be hurt. It had become part of her identity so that, even though she declared forgiveness for those who hurt her, this spirit didn't seem to want to leave. It had woven itself into her identity and she didn't know who she would be without it. It was familiar—unwanted, but familiar. It was her normal.

She, like the previous person, needed to displace the darkness. They both needed not only to expose the lies they had believed but to embrace their true identity. Once people know who they really are, they are able to manifest the authority they have in Jesus to intentionally remove the false identity they have embraced. In the case of these two women, agreement with the embedded lies that fabricated their identity actually gave the demons permission to stay. Though I didn't work either of them through a displacement process, I have helped others in this same dilemma displace the darkness and emerge into lasting freedom.

For those who need to displace the darkness, I recommend that you follow the process designed to rebuild a godly stronghold described in the next few chapters. It is not only good for those who are filling up their lives with a godly stronghold, but it is also very effective in displacing darkness as you uncover and remove lies, embracing your true identity even as you destroy the false one.

The Mystery

I can pretty much discern if the two previous conditions are present and the work that needs to be done. However, there are those very rare times that I am just in a quandary about what to do because nothing works. Those are very rare and I have no choice except to file them in the mystery category. I know there is a cause but my discernment is not picking up on what to do next.

On one of those occasions my team and I had been ministering to a lady, but nothing we did seemed to work. The woman had shut every open door she knew of, and in my conversations with the Holy Spirit I could not discern anything else. We ministered like this for a couple of hours when I finally prayed, "Lord, I'm at a loss about what to do. Would You just come and free this woman?"

In the next few minutes the glory of the Lord flooded the room. It was a scary experience for me, a tangible presence of His holiness. At that moment I forgot about everyone else in the room and thought, "You guys are on your own this time!" as I hit the floor and started confessing every sin I could recall. His holy presence was so tangible it was as if light shone on every bit of darkness in my life. While in my own little world dealing with my stuff, the woman remained seated in her chair as the Lord filled her and flushed out that stubborn spirit. Soon she began to prophesy over us with extreme accuracy that encouraged all of us. She was a changed woman after that encounter. Not only was she set free but she began to regularly and clearly hear the Lord's voice.

If you aren't getting anywhere, why not just ask the Holy Spirit to come and do for them what you can't?

Part 2

STAYING FREE

Chapter 8

───────

DO YOU HAVE A PLAN
TO STAY FREE?

I DID MY DOCTORAL DISSERTATION ON POST-DELIVERANCE discipleship. My research examined the positive factors that enable a person to successfully steward his freedom after deliverance ministry, and identified which negative factors contribute to his slipping back into bondage. I discovered two primary factors that contribute to ongoing freedom. If *either one* of these factors is present, the person's chances of maintaining his healing and freedom are very good.

The first crucial factor is having a support system in place. More than just attending church, this kind of support system means living in relational community with others who can and will speak into the individual's life and help him through the challenges inherent in walking out his freedom. Those who successfully maintained their freedom were committed to making the support system work, willing to stick it out and not run off or quit when things got difficult. Understanding the power of living in community is a primary motivating factor for remaining in relationship. Finding a community that will stick with the person as he learns to live according to

God's truth instead of the enemy's lies, even when things get ugly, isn't always easy. But it is absolutely possible if the individual will continue to ask and seek the Lord's direction.

In today's culture many believers practice a consumer-based Christianity where they refuse to be plugged into a fellowship but, instead, go from church to church looking for the intangible perfect mix. This kind of gypsy fellowshipping comes at the cost of missing the very qualities necessary for victorious living. Successfully maintaining the freedom gained from deliverance ministry means the person must be rooted in a church family that will provide accountability, love, discipleship, kindness, and will stick with him all the way through the restoration process.

The second factor that I identified in people who successfully maintained their freedom after deliverance was having a specific plan or a process to follow in the days and weeks after ministry. Sadly, because it is such a deficiency in most deliverance ministries, few people received a "what to do after ministry" plan from those who led them into freedom. Even in the plethora of deliverance books I read, only a handful devoted time or attention to a follow-up process. For those I surveyed who had and followed a plan, it often resulted from their relationships, through a discipleship plan from their church, or through a Bible study with some friends. What most amazed me, although I shouldn't have been surprised, was the way that the Holy Spirit always provided a plan for those who diligently sought one. It might not have fallen into their lap, but if they looked for a plan or process to follow, they got one. Those who seek will certainly find.

The very good news from my research is that if either one of these two factors was present in the seeker's life, having a support system or having a plan, his chances of stewarding that newfound freedom into a victorious life were good. If both factors were present, his chances were great!

The New Testament doesn't offer many long-term post deliverance case studies, but it seems clear that the objective was to get rid of the demons and then go on with life. Scripture records only a few individuals who experienced deliverance even though there were hundreds (possibly even thousands) more who were rid of their demons. Unfortunately we don't know the rest of their story. Mary Magdalene, who had seven demons cast out of her (Mark 16:9), is the exception. Her "aftercare" was hanging around Jesus. By this lack we might be tempted to conclude that after-care was a non-issue, except for an intriguing passage in which Jesus discusses an important truth directly relevant to what happens after deliverance. Jesus said in Matthew 12:43-45:

> *Now when the unclean spirit goes out of a man, it passes through waterless places seeking rest, and does not find it. Then it says, "I will return to my house from which I came"; and when it comes, it finds it unoccupied, swept, and put in order. Then it goes and takes along with it seven other spirits more wicked than itself, and they go in and live there; and the last state of that man becomes worse than the first. That is the way it will also be with this evil generation.*

The alarming portion states that if the house (a person's life) is left unoccupied, swept, and put in order there is a danger that the latter condition could potentially become worse than the first. When a demon leaves its home, it wants to come back. Swept and put in order are certainly good things, but being left empty seems to be the major problem. If nothing comes in to occupy the emptied places that demon inhabited, it is possible the person might become more demonized after ministry than he was before. The issue is this: How can a person occupy his life so that there remains no room or opportunity for the demonic to reenter those clean swept places? If a person has gone through deliverance from the influence of a demonic spirit, how does he retain that freedom?

Experience has revealed that most people who get rid of the demonic fill their house with Jesus as a result of their normal Christian walk. Worship, reading scriptures, and fellowshipping with other believers leave little room for the enemy to return with seven worse than itself. The aftercare for many who had been demonically oppressed is simply the pursuit of spiritual maturity by walking daily with Jesus. Experience has also revealed that, with others, more is required to sustain freedom. It is heartbreaking to see someone experience such great freedom only to find himself back in bondage and, in many cases, fulfill the scripture where the latter condition is worse than the previous one.

How do you know if you are the person requiring more intense follow-up effort to stay free? That is a great question with no exact answer. What I have observed is that it is often dependent upon how ingrained the demonic thinking is into what you consider your normal thought patterns. Are any thoughts or thinking patterns in agreement with the demonic lies? The more your thought structures agree with any area of bondage, the more attention you should give to dismantling them. The demon might have been expelled but the work really isn't complete until the thought structures that supported that demon are dismantled and new ones, which are in agreement with freedom, are intentionally built in that place.

If you have made it to this part of the book you are either wanting to help someone who needs to stay free, you need to stay free yourself, or you have a spirit intertwined in your identity that needs to be displaced. In the next few chapters I will be talking to you as if you are the person who wants to rebuild a stronghold of righteousness.

Chapter 9

STRONGHOLDS

GRASPING THE BIBLICAL CONCEPT OF A "STRONGHOLD" WILL be helpful as you come out of bondage and into freedom. It is a term pulled out of Second Corinthians 10:3-5, which we will examine in a moment. A stronghold can be defined as an ingrained repetitive thinking process which your mind regularly travels down. What you think determines how you see yourself, how you see others, and how you see your world. Thoughts lead to feelings and feelings determine behavior. To break it down simply: your beliefs determine what you feel and what you feel motivates what you do. You do what you feel like doing. If you want to change what you do, then you need to change your feelings. Unfortunately, that isn't always as simple as it sounds.

Even though you cannot change your feelings, you can change your beliefs, which determine your thoughts. Changing your thoughts will change your feelings and that will, in turn, impact your actions. What your mind and your thoughts gravitate to determine how you feel, how you live, and who you will become. For our purposes, let's define a stronghold as a dominating thought pattern that rules how you think, how you respond, and determines your behaviors. Strongholds can either be godly or ungodly, righteous or unrighteous. Your thought patterns can either bring you into life or bring you into ruin.

You may not realize this but there is an adversary who has a "scheme" against you (2 Cor. 2:11; Eph. 6:11). Your ignorance of that scheme will divert you from your divine destiny by giving you an alternative identity and an alternative destiny. That alternate identity may have started operating when you were a child. Your enemy whispered a lie that you embraced as true. You thought about that lie over and over until it became your normal thought pattern. You didn't realize that the adversary was shaping your thinking as you continually embraced the lies that he whispered to your mind. Because you have repetitively thought these thoughts, the lies feel like truth. Once they feel true, they become part of your identity. Thus, you have embraced an alternative identity that you actually believe is the real you. In actuality, it is a counterfeit from the schemer to derail you from your divine destiny, to prevent you from becoming the person God intended you to be. This tactic successfully separates some people from their true destiny. In others, it limits their potential by constraining what is possible. Sadly, some have been seduced by these deceiving spirits their whole life and are now in bondage to an alternative identity that feels normal to them. This alternative identity and alternative destiny may fit into the world's view of success but it misses that person's divine destiny, which has eternal impact.

Going down those alternative thought patterns repetitively entrenches them in your mind like ruts or grooves on a dirt road. My grandpa owned a dairy farm, which I loved visiting when I was young. He milked those cows twice a day. They were in a pen for the evening, but after the early morning milking they were turned out to pasture. In mid-afternoon he hopped in his pickup and went into the field, honking the horn, and those cows came in to get milked. Cows are easily trained. The road he went down was dirt and he went down that road so many times that he had worn deep grooves in it. It seemed like he really didn't need to steer much, just set the tires in the grooves and hit the accelerator. When a cow had a calf, though, he would have to get out of the grooves and head across the pasture to pick up the calf and put it in the back of the pickup, otherwise momma cow would not come to the barn.

That is a great picture of the human mind. You go down those thoughts until you wear grooves. If this happens often enough, those faulty pathways become your normal default thinking. Your default thinking is where you naturally gravitate if left unchecked. However, there is a thinking pattern that is in agreement with heaven and that is what you need to embrace. You must get out of the ruts and cut a new road. Then you need to go down it often enough to create new grooves that become your new default thinking. You can fill in the old ruts and create new ones, but you have to go down the new ones enough times that they will feel normal to you. Until that time you will still have old default thinking patterns that feel more normal to you than the new ones.

Some of those old default thinking patterns are based on lies and become an ungodly stronghold that rules your life. You become a slave to your thoughts, so that they control you, rather than you controlling your thoughts. You then have an unrighteous thinking process that rules, controls, and dominates your thoughts, dictating unrighteous behaviors. Second Corinthians 10 says:

> *For though we live in the world, we do not wage war as*
> *the world does. The weapons we fight with are not the*

weapons of the world. On the contrary, they have divine power to demolish strongholds. We demolish arguments and every pretension that sets itself up against the knowledge of God, and we take captive every thought to make it obedient to Christ (2 Corinthians 10:3-5 NIV).

You must engage in spiritual battle to tear down and demolish ungodly strongholds. Demonic strongholds are those ingrained thought patterns that are raised up against the knowledge of God, disobedient thoughts that have not been taken captive. When unhindered, unrighteous thinking rules; it gives way to further thoughts that are in direct opposition to the character and will of God. If not addressed, those areas eventually become your master and will determine how you think and feel. Even though you may succeed in temporarily pushing wrongful thoughts to the background of your mind rather than the forefront, if not dismantled and removed they can still surface and negatively impact your life. You have to dismantle the old default thinking, rebuild a new thought system, and repeatedly travel down it enough to create deep grooves that will sustain the new, godly stronghold.

When ungodly strongholds rule your thought life, the structures they establish can become the support system for demonic spirits. Any ungodly house of thoughts, built of lies and wounds, attracts and shelters demonic spirits. Unrighteous thinking systems agree with darkness, and that kind of agreement empowers the enemy. The problem is that you have entertained those thoughts so long they seem normal to you. Once deliverance has occurred, you must dismantle the old thought patterns and build new ones that agree with your new nature and your true destiny.

On rare occasions I have seen someone who not only got free of their demons, but all of those old thinking patterns associated with that demonic spirit were totally obliterated as well. I wish this happened to every person who was delivered, but it typically does not work that way. Some who have experienced that kind of immediate freedom often think their experience is normative. I wish it were, but for most of us there is no delete button for our thoughts.

Here is the good news! When you gave your life to Jesus you were made into a new creature, reconnected to God through the Holy Spirit. In this divine connection, because of Jesus indwelling you through the Holy Spirit, you have the mind of Christ (1 Cor. 2:16). Jesus' mind is available to you! However, just because it is available to you doesn't mean your thoughts are always in tune with His thoughts. Romans 12:2 says new-creation believers are transformed by the renewing of their mind. Just because you are a new creation doesn't mean you have a renewed mind. It does mean that you have access to heavenly thinking, the mind of Christ, which you did not as an unbeliever. You must pursue the heavenly thinking now available to you. That's why Paul tells the church in Colossians 3:2-3 to set their minds on things above and, in Philippians 4:8, what their minds should dwell on. As a new creation you have access to heavenly thinking, but that doesn't mean it is automatic. A new creation doesn't mean you are transformed. You must cooperate with what God put in you and go through the transformation process by the renewing of your mind. *"And do not be conformed to this world, but be transformed by the renewing of your mind, so that you may prove what the will of God is, that which is good and acceptable and perfect"* (Rom. 12:2).

Once a person is free from evil spirits he needs to assess his thought processes. Are they godly or ungodly? Do they agree with truth or lies? Some will feel immediate relief right after the demonic expulsion with no apparent residue of the departed demonic spirit. Others may feel dazed and a bit numb, as if something familiar is now gone, aware of an emptiness in the place the spirit vacated. After deliverance, awareness of your new freedom will dominate your thoughts. As time goes on, you must continually evaluate whether your thoughts are continuing to flow in agreement with your freedom or reverting back to thoughts of bondage. Keep asking yourself, *What feels true* or *What do I feel like doing*? Often that prodding that you felt to do wrong things came from those harassing demonic spirits. With those spirits gone the urge should have lifted. If that thinking structure isn't going through renewal, however, you may continue to pursue those old patterns because that kind of thinking feels normal to you. If this happens, it may keep the door open for something to return.

As I mentioned earlier, most individuals who go through deliverance from demonic influences can adequately occupy their life through a normal Christian walk with Jesus. You don't always know how the demons got in—what legal right opened the door, whether or not they were invited, or if they were just intruders. Oftentimes you just get them out when you come across them. Most believers do just fine as they are filled with the Holy Spirit, enjoy the presence of God in worship, fill their life with the Word of God, and fellowship with other believers. But if you have cooperated with that demonic spirit (probably unknowingly) and developed a thought structure that gave the spirit authority in your life, it may be necessary to intentionally rebuild that area with a godly stronghold in the opposite spirit of the one you cast out. This will ensure the demonic cannot take further advantage of you. Paul told the believers at Corinth not to be ignorant of the devil's schemes: *"so that no advantage would be taken of us by Satan, for we are not ignorant of his schemes"* (2 Cor. 2:11). You are not warring against flesh and blood (Eph. 6) and must be diligent and wise as you fight this good fight.

What does it look like to rebuild in the opposite spirit? The following chart lists typical ungodly strongholds on the left with a corresponding righteous stronghold on the right:

UNGODLY STRONGHOLD	GODLY STRONGHOLD
pride/self-promotion	humility
self-hate	self-acceptance/love
rejection	acceptance
lust/greed	contentment
hate	love
fear	trust
depression	joy
anxiety	peace
bitterness	compassion
rage	self-control
rebellion	submission

This is not an exhaustive list nor an exact science. Depending on the variables of the negative stronghold, you may need to adjust the exact stronghold you want to rebuild in its place. For example, if you struggle with fear, what kind of fear is it? Is it a fear of man, fear of failure, fear of the devil, fear of being alone, or some other kind of fear? The opposite could be a stronghold of faith, a stronghold of courage or boldness, or something else that confronts that particular fear. Identifying the strongholds that once disabled you will clearly indicate what you must intentionally tear down and which godly stronghold to rebuild in its place. Here is the really good news: the devil fears godly virtue. It erases his work and releases the authority of heaven in a person's life.

Chapter 10

THE POWER OF GOD'S WORD

I HAVE INCLUDED SCRIPTURE REFERENCES THROUGHOUT this book because I am convinced about the great power in God's Word. As you move into freedom, it helps tremendously to know how to invoke that power as a source of strength and for direction. Building a stronghold of righteousness will require you to get into the scriptures and study them.

There is nothing like digging in the Word of God and finding out for yourself what God has to say about who He really is and who you really are. The Bible claims that scripture is authoritative for life. The Bible claims it has the right to determine what is truth and what is not truth. For you see, only God can determine truth. We all need something that is outside of our subjective feelings, an objective source of truth. That objective source is the Bible.

> *But know this first of all, that no prophecy of Scripture is a matter of one's own interpretation, for no prophecy was ever made by an act of human will, but men moved by the Holy Spirit spoke from God* (2 Peter 1:20-21).

The biblical authors didn't just write what they wanted. Neither were they in some robotic trance as they wrote, without their mind or personality. God poured His Word through them keeping their personality intact, yet what they wrote was completely inspired by God and brought life! Man didn't think this up! It was purely God.

Relationship is more than just knowing about someone. You can know a lot about President Lincoln but you haven't met him. He's been gone a long time. You can know a lot about President George Washington, but you don't know him. It is important not to confuse knowledge about someone with personal knowledge, which only comes with relationship. You can know about God but not really know God. He not only wants us to know about Him, but to have a personal knowledge of Him as well. Scripture reveals and points, but it is not an end unto itself. Knowing scripture is not supposed to be the object of your life—knowing God is! The purpose of scripture is to point to God through Christ, the revealed Word.

And the Father who sent Me, He has testified of Me. You have neither heard His voice at any time, nor seen His form. You do not have His word abiding in you, for you do not believe Him whom He sent. You search the Scriptures because you think that in them you have eternal life; it is these that testify about Me; and you are unwilling to come to Me so that you may have life (John 5:37-40).

In this passage Jesus spoke to the Pharisees, who knew the Old Testament scripture. Jesus said that they searched the scripture because they thought there was life in the scripture. He implied that life is found only in Him about whom the scripture spoke. Life is found in Christ. The role of God's Word is to point to the source of life—Jesus!

Do you know what makes scripture so powerful? It is the living God who is in scripture, not the book itself. The Bible would be absolutely powerless and just plain ordinary if God didn't infuse the words with power. The reason the book contains power is because God empowers it. God empowers it because it points to Him!

Encountering God through scripture will change you. But you must encounter the God of the Word when you come to the Word of God if you want to be changed. The Pharisees encountered the Word of God, but missed the God of the Word. They sought life in scripture rather than in Jesus, the giver of life. You could do the same thing if you are not careful. What impacts and changes your life is an encounter with Christ.

Hebrews 12:2 says, *"fixing our eyes on Jesus, the author and perfecter of faith."* Jesus is the author and perfecter of our faith. The scripture is simply the tool that God uses to reveal Himself to you and reveal the truth about you. Jesus is the one who changes lives and God will use the revelation of truth in the Word of God to do it.

The Bible claims to be the Word of Truth (2 Tim. 2:15). It is the final authority for truth in our world today. Your success in spiritual warfare, your capacity to live in victory and experience the abundant life, begins with your acceptance of the Word of God as the sole and final authority of what is truth and what is error. Your standard for truth cannot be the wisdom of man. It cannot be human reason, because the things of God go beyond human wisdom and reason (1 Cor. 2:14).

We are subjective creatures that need objective input. *Subjective* means the things that I sense and feel. God made us creatures with feelings, emotions, and perceptions. I see and live through my past experiences and the things that have made me who I am. As a result we tend to have certain prejudices. So the word *subjective* basically means "How I see things, how I perceive things, or how I feel." *Objective* describes something outside of myself, a thing not based on experiences or feelings.

You must be able to stand on something outside of yourself and that can only be the Word of God. If something is objective, it must be outside of ourselves. We need something that is outside of our subjective feelings that can speak objectively into our lives. The Bible is that and does that.

> *For the word of God is living and active and sharper than any two-edged sword, and piercing as far as the division of soul and spirit, of both joints and marrow, and able to judge the thoughts and intentions of the heart* (Hebrews 4:12).

Let's say that you and a friend disagree. You argue over something that probably is trivial. Your feelings and emotions are wrapped up in the issue and your view of reality is skewed, or prejudiced, by those feelings. You are so involved in the issue you cannot see things clearly even though you think you can. Your friend is in the same predicament. Both of you view the situation *subjectively*, from an inside perspective. You both have to go to another person, a third party, to assist in settling the dispute. You choose to go to someone who was not involved in the dispute and who can be *objective*, who can look at the situation from an outside perspective.

It is like two people going to court to let a judge settle an issue. The judge is not involved and will render an objective opinion. Going to a third party enables someone outside of the issue who does not have subjective feelings or involvement to make a rational judgment.

That is what the Bible should be to you. You must recognize that you see things from a subjective perspective. Your thinking, judgments, perceptions, and vision are based on what is going on within you. As a result, you don't always see things clearly. You don't know truth completely because your mind is tainted by your environment and experiences. You need truth that is not founded upon your subjective feelings, but is based on what is outside of yourself. Real truth, by its nature, is objective. That is what you need to guide you as you rebuild godly strongholds, and that is the role of the Bible.

For example, God says in His Word that He loves us. However, you may not feel loved. You may have had a cruel earthly father who mistreated you, or perhaps your earthly father died when you were young so you don't understand a father's love. You may have had a father who never spent time with you and so you never sensed love from your earthly father. That taints your perspective of God, our heavenly Father. If you can't find love from an earthly father you can see, how can you receive love from a heavenly Father you can't see? Because of your past experiences you might feel that you are not loved and so can't fully comprehend that God loves you. However, the Bible tells us over and over how God loves us. This truth is not based on your experiences (your subjective feelings), it is based on the objective Word of God. Truth is truth, regardless of how you feel about something. Your thoughts and feelings do not make something true. God's Word gives you real truth that is not based on your feelings.

Because the Word of God is the revelation of God, you can know about God through it. The Word of God reveals the nature of God. You can know what He is really like through His Word. Regardless of your experience, you can know God's true nature through His Word. His character is revealed through His acts. His nature is revealed. His grace, His love, His passions are all spelled out in His Word.

Scripture reveals the ways of God. Learning about God is the beginning point of a relationship, but knowing His ways enables you to know Him better.

> *Now therefore, I pray thee, if I have found grace in thy*
> *sight, shew me now thy way, that I may know thee, that*
> *I may find grace in thy sight: and consider that this*
> *nation is thy people* (Exodus 33:13 KJV).

When Moses wanted to know the Lord, he sought to know God's ways. If you know His ways, you know Him. By studying the Word, you can know God's ways and how He operates. You can know His provision and how to cooperate with Him for His provision. You can know God's promises. Scripture will even reveal God's plans.

You can know about yourself. What are you really like? What is the truth about your life? What is the truth about your future? What is the truth about your condition? In the Word you can know the truth regarding righteousness and how you stack up against it—what is right and what is wrong. The Word reveals who you really are in Christ and who you are apart from Christ. The Word of God reveals your future. It will even unveil the condition of the heart.

These are all the reasons you absolutely need the truth to combat the lies of the evil one as you walk out and steward your freedom.

Truth guards against the adversary's most effective weapons. Truth counteracts deception. Satan's ultimate desire is to deceive man.

> *For you are the children of your father the devil, and you love to do the evil things he does. He was a murderer from the beginning. He has always hated the truth, because there is no truth in him. When he lies, it is consistent with his character; for he is a liar and the father of lies* (John 8:44 NLT).

The Word of God devastates and totally defeats satan and the demonic spirits that make up his kingdom. It exposes their deceitful and lying ways and breaks their power against you, the believer.

Since the cross of Christ totally defeated the devil, the only effective weapon he has is the weapon of deception. He deceives his way to power. He usurps power when you agree with his lies, which means he only has the power that you give him. He can only defeat you if you let him. The key to overcoming the devil is to draw from the reservoir of truth that abides in you. Hearing and doing the Word of God builds a strong foundation of truth within you.

The key to being strong and continually conquering the evil one is proportional to the measure that the Word of God abides in you. God has given us His Word in the Bible and how seriously you take it and put it into practice will have a direct effect on your ability to consistently live in strength and victory.

> *All Scripture is inspired by God and profitable for teaching, for reproof, for correction, for training in righteousness; so that the man of God may be adequate, equipped for every good work* (2 Timothy 3:16-17).

Let the power of God's Word impact your life. If you will do the work, digging out the truths in God's Word for the godly character you want to build into your life, you will have a biblical foundation upon which you can stand victoriously. However, knowing what God says isn't enough. You must be a "doer of the Word," putting into practice what you have learned (James 1:22-24).

Chapter 11

THE REMOVING AND THE REBUILDING PROCESS

TEARING DOWN AN OLD DEMONIC ABODE AND REBUILDING A godly stronghold in that place is an intentional, multi-step process that benefits those who have already come into freedom, as well as those who are still pursuing freedom as they actively displace darkness. This process involves removing any legal rights that enable the enemy to put you into bondage, burning bridges so you cannot return to any old areas of darkness, taking back your true identity, and rebuilding a stronghold of godliness in that place. Some of this work is accomplished as you are set free of demonic influence. However, it doesn't hurt go back through some of these areas to be thorough and reinforce what you've done. Going through the rebuilding steps more than once isn't redundant, but will accomplish a thorough housecleaning as you mop up any residue and reinforce your liberty, leaving no room for the demonic to return.

Step 1: Identify and Confess Your Sins

Freedom begins as you recognize and/or acknowledge how the enemy entrapped you. Were you enticed through greed, addiction, or lust? Did you succumb to anger, jealousy, or bitterness? Did the enemy sideline you through fear or rejection? Whatever area of bondage caused you to think thoughts that were not in agreement with God, and to do things not in tune with His will, must be identified. Getting free and staying free requires you to come into agreement with God and see things as He sees them. Thinking ungodly thoughts and doing ungodly activities are both sin. Acknowledgement means that you admit you have sinned and confess it to God. *Confession* means to come into agreement with God. You must see it as God sees it. What happens when you confess?

First John 1:9 says, *"If we confess our sins, He is faithful and righteous to forgive us our sins and to cleanse us from all unrighteousness."*

Why is this important? Because grace flows when you are in tune with God. Confessing your sins means you agree with God—you see your sin as God sees it. When you see things the way that God sees things, you position yourself to walk in the fullness of His grace and power. This means that you don't diminish sin's significance or the power it had over your life. It means that you don't belittle it or declare that it is not that big of a deal. You see it as God sees it. You see it as having thwarted God's will for your life. You see it as a place that entrapped you and kept you from your destiny. You see it from the perspective that it was so significant Jesus died to heal it. The rebuilding process ensures that you do what is necessary to see everything as Jesus sees it. This creates a foundation upon which you can build a place of godly occupation and strength.

You can claim this promise when you bring things to the light and confess them for what they are. *"He who conceals his transgressions will not prosper, but he who confesses and forsakes them will find compassion"* (Prov. 28:13).

Step 2: Thoroughly Remove Every Legal Right

You must revoke a spirit's legal right to remain before you can begin to regain what's been lost. Even though some demons leave when commanded, others do not leave until their legal right has been renounced and canceled. You revoke any legal right the demon perceives it has and retake that ground.

Here is how you renounce, or revoke, demonic legal rights. Ask the Holy Spirit if there is any remaining legal right that you have not thoroughly addressed. As you do this, listen carefully and expect an answer! Hearing God's voice might be a little new to you but often you can tell if it is God's voice or not. If the thoughts that come to your mind are negative, demeaning, shaming, or self-condemning, then you are definitely listening to the wrong channel. The Holy Spirit will bring light but will avoid condemnation. He will convict but not condemn. So just take some time right now, be still a moment, and ask the Holy Spirit to search your heart and see if there is any real estate that has been surrendered that needs to be taken back. His thoughts tend to merge with your thoughts, so it might feel like what pops up originated in your own mind, but pay attention to the affirmation of His Spirit who resides in you.

When you ask the Holy Spirit to look into your heart, He might reveal a bridge to the old sin that's still intact. Even though you know you need to, you haven't burned it yet. Sometimes those bridges are hard to burn because there is that lingering thought in the back of your mind that doing so feels a little too permanent. Those aren't your thoughts that want to keep those bridges intact! Burning the bridges that connect you to any sort of sin is necessary so you won't be tempted to return to the old habits, actions, and choices. When I got married, I made sure that I didn't keep any pictures of previous girlfriends. I wasn't returning to any of them so I didn't need to keep them. You now must rid your life of any residue or reminder of that bondage. You have to change playgrounds and change playmates if you haven't done so already. This is what it looks like, what it will take, to remove any legal right that might enable the demons to return.

This step will reveal your true motives. Many times people remove an area of bondage because it is painful and/or problematic in their life. However, the thought of burning the bridges, never, ever to return, can be extremely difficult. Calling on God's power to reinforce the eviction notice and determining never to return is a permanent decision that requires a strong commitment. What does your heart really want to do? Are you willing to make a genuine, permanent commitment to burn every bridge or are you just ridding yourself of an inconvenience you might want to entertain later? Getting truly free will depend on how you answer that question. Staying free will depend on how thoroughly you identify and remove legal rights and then burn every bridge.

Step 3: Repent

You have to really grasp and practice repentance. Repentance is significant because it was the central message of John the Baptist as he prepared the way for the Messiah, of Jesus, as He brought the Kingdom of God, and the central message at the birth of the church (Matt. 3:2; 4:17; Acts 2:38; 3:19). Unfortunately, it has been much maligned and given a negative label because of being wrongly associated with fire and brimstone preaching.

Repentance has to become a lifestyle, not just an event. Repentance simply means to change your mind. Repentance is a lifestyle of daily aligning your thoughts with God's thoughts. One issue that many face is that you must repent (change your thinking) from a cultural religious perception of repentance to God's view of repentance. It's not "turning from your evil ways." It is changing your mind to be in agreement with heaven.

Repentance Is Not...

Repentance is not remorse. You might feel remorse before you choose to repent. Remorse is often the first step toward repentance. It involves feeling bad for what you have done, feeling sorry, and possibly wishing it hadn't happened. The Bible talks about godly sorrow that produces repentance (2 Cor. 7:9-12), but remorse is just sorrow over something you wish had not happened. Repentance is more than remorse. It is not just feeling bad about what has happened. It is not just wishing that you had not done what you did. Remorse may lead to repentance, but don't think you have repented just because you felt remorse.

Repentance is not regret. Regret is wishing you hadn't done something.[1] We all feel remorse and regret when we experience the conviction of the Holy Spirit after we do wrong. We may suffer condemnation from the adversary as well. Regret is wishing you could go back and do it over. Regret may lead to repentance, but wishing you could go back and undo it is not repentance. The prodigal son had remorse and regret for the decisions he made, but repentance happened when he came to his senses and decided to return to his father's house.

Repentance is not reform, though it may look like it from the outside. Reform is just straightening up your life in the sense of doing good things to find acceptability, but it is not repentance. Becoming religious is not repentance. You can start the right activities and not have a true heart change. When people hear they must repent to be saved, they interpret that to mean they have to *get their act together* or *reform* before they can come to Jesus. Repentance is a part of receiving salvation, but repentance isn't just becoming religious and doing religious things. Genuine repentance will result in action, but the action will concur with a change that has already taken place on the inside—in the mind.

What Repentance Is

Repentance means "change." Repentance comes from the Greek word *metanoia*, which means "change" or "change your mind." It is a change of the mind. Actions are the fruit of repentance. A changed mind should result in changed actions, but the beginning step happens in the mind. This mental change is to be an act of your will. Actions are the indicator that genuine repentance has taken place (Luke 3:7). If actions don't result, repentance is probably not genuine.

Having agreed with God through confession, you are now ready to change your mind and that should result in a change of your life. You examine your life to see if there is any "right" remaining and choose to permanently cut it off. You are taking back what has been stolen. You are asking God to help burn your bridges, never to return. Repentance means to stop wrong thinking, embrace right thinking, and begin the journey from bondage toward righteousness.

Step 4: Replace the Lies with Truth

Next you must identify the lies you have embraced, remove them, and replace them with God's truth. To do this you are going to dismantle old thought patterns and replace them with new ones. You are giving Jesus, your new landlord, remodeling rights over these regained areas. He wants to rip out the old structure so He can build a new one. The only way to destroy the old structure is to bring your mind into submission to God's Word. You are then able to confront the thought patterns that have ruled you and counter them with the truth and power of the Word of God.

A practical way to do this is to make a list with two columns. In the column on the left, list wrongful thoughts that are getting exposed. These are usually lies you have believed that reinforced wrong thinking. As you do this, don't allow shame or embarrassment to tempt you to be less than honest. Pride might try to prevent total disclosure. Don't be surprised if you find yourself verbalizing, for the first time things that ruled your thoughts and reveal how you actually felt. (An example of lies is found in Appendix B.)

Now that you have identified and listed the lies, it's time to counter them with truth. The right-hand column is for the truth. Search God's Word (the Bible) and begin to build a list of God's truth that refutes each lie. (A list of truths is listed in Appendix C and Appendix D.) Select truths that specifically speak into your true identity—the truth regarding your destiny, the truth about God, the truth of how God really sees you, and the truth of how God chooses to relate to you. You must assault those old thought patterns with the truth found in God's Word. This list of truths will form the foundation for an identity statement that you are going to develop, one which you can daily speak over your life to renew your mind and reinforce God's truth.

If you are having trouble identifying the lies, there are some practical ways to get started. Go to Appendix D and look at the truths of who you are and some examples of truths about God. Mark the ones that feel true and the ones that don't feel true. Intellectually you will recognize most of them and agree that they are true. But this step isn't about what you know in your head; it is all about how you feel. Those that don't feel true have, at their core, a lie you have embraced. Don't feel ashamed about what you are discovering. You are in the process of exposing something that the enemy has used to disable you. This is a good thing! Make your list with lies on the left and truths on the right. The lies will expose the stronghold of darkness, and the truths you want to embrace will shift your core beliefs.

Another way to identify the lies is to work your way backward from your unwanted actions to come to the lie. Remember that your core beliefs produce thoughts. Thoughts produce emotions and emotions influence how you act. Your activities flow from how you feel. The truth is, you do what you want to do because you feel like doing it. Those feelings flow from your thoughts that have a core belief. Start with the unwanted action. *What did you do? Why did you do it?* Then move to the feeling. *What were you feeling when you did it?* Now you can ponder what you were thinking. *What did you believe to be true that made you feel that way?*

Step 5: Exchange the False Identity with Your True Identity

As you identify the lies you have embraced, you are also going to begin to identify any place you have accepted a false identity. Wherever one of these lies has determined how you see yourself, lies you have believed were true, these will become a false identity. You must replace any false identity with the truth of who you really are. In this step you are answering the question, "Who is the real me?" Your true self is the one based on the truth from the Word of God. This truth will differentiate who you are from who you aren't. As we have learned, negative strongholds will alter your thinking, behavior, and emotions. They can become so ingrained you actually believe you have become that person. It is how you see yourself.

Your true identity is only found in how God sees you, not in your previous thought systems, your activities, or how you feel. It is found in God who made you and in the freedom that you find in Christ. Living in freedom requires you to identify the areas you have embraced in your perceived identity that aren't the "real" you, regardless of how true they may feel. These areas must be recognized as a false identity, revealing how you became someone else rather than who you really are. Our true identity can only be found in Christ. Therefore, you must repent of these false identities and embrace who you are in Christ.

In rebuilding your thought life you must be willing to clearly identify the thoughts, emotions, and behaviors that you embraced as your identity. Recognizing these, putting a name to them, helps you put on the brakes when you go down that wrong road. This knowledge enables you more easily to stop and say, "Hey! That's not who I am! I don't have to put up with that anymore!" It becomes a tool that the Holy Spirit can use to remind you, "You don't have to do this... You don't have to think this way... You don't have to react like this... You don't have to live like this...."

Having identified lies and truth, it's time to examine how the lies became a part of how you see yourself or how you think others perceive you. Make another pair of columns. On the left side, list the false identity that you have embraced and on the right, list your true identity, who the Bible says you really are. On the false-identity side, you can start with a short list of what you know you used to do, think, or feel and on the other side, write what you are now free to do, think, or feel. The false identity can be: how you see yourself, a reaction you have, a fear you possess, a struggle you have relating to others, a wall that you set up to protect yourself, an ungodly lifestyle, a negative tendency in your character, or a sin you keep repeating. (A list of examples of false identities is found in Appendix E.) Confess to God your part in taking on this false identity. Repent and renounce that false identity and then declare your true identity, who you really are in Christ! Write out the truth regarding who God says you are! It is fine to begin with a short list, but, as time goes on, don't be surprised if the list grows as you uncover more things about who you aren't and who you are. In fact, give yourself plenty of time because the list of who you really are is really long. God loves telling us how He sees us and it is all wonderful!

Step 6: Research the Righteous Stronghold(s) You Want in Your Life

Once you know the righteous stronghold(s) you want to build into your life, it is time to do some more work and get into God's Word yourself and research it. I know this sounds like a lot of effort, and it is, but all your exploration is doing wonders for your soul and feeding your spirit. Even if your brain isn't fully comprehending things, your spirit is. I recommend doing a character Bible study. Study the righteous character you want to put into your life. It may seem tedious at times as you look at a ton of scripture making your brain swim, but none of the time invested is time wasted. I took a character Bible study method that I found in Rick Warren's book, *Personal Bible Study Methods*, and adjusted it a bit. It is found in Appendix F. As you do your study, lay out the truths and scripture that resonates with you! From those you can create your identity statement.

Step 7: Create a Unique Personal Identity Statement

If you meditate on the truths of who you are based on the Word of God, transformation will occur as the mind is renewed (Rom. 12:2). Meditation is to dwell over and over on the truths of God. The one who meditates on the ways of God will be like a tree planted by a river that has a continual supply of nourishment (Ps.1:2-3) and drives His Word deep, which keeps them walking in God's ways and not walking in sin (Ps. 119:11). There are many ways to meditate on His Word. You can make a list of verses that speak into your true identity and read those out loud every day until they become second nature to your thinking. You can even memorize a few that seem most important for your transition. Another way is to create an identity statement that includes the truths of who you are but may be written out in either a declaration you pronounce over yourself or as a conversation that God would say to you. The identity statement agrees with the godly stronghold of righteousness that you are building into your life.

I am a real fan of declarations. There is something about the power of words released over us that, when in agreement with the Word of God and the will of God, empowers us. We know from James 3 that words have such substance that they determine the direction of our lives like a bit in a horse's mouth or a rudder on a ship (James 3:3-4). Our words contain the power to curse and the power to bless. When our words are in agreement with the will of God, they release grace for the fulfillment of heaven's assignments, empowering the angels, as our authority to bind and loose is unleashed toward God's purposes. That is what an identity statement does when, after it has been regularly declared over you, it becomes your own.

Create an identity statement that is uniquely yours. Include in it the uniqueness of your true identity. Say it over yourself every day and let the truth of God's Word sink into your spirit. Some examples of identity statements are found in Appendix G.

Endnote

1. Some translations say that Judas "repented" (felt bad) for what he did by betraying Jesus in Matthew 27:3. This is not the same word that is used by John the Baptist in Matthew 3:2 or with Jesus in Matthew 4:17. The word used with Judas is *metamellomai*—"to regret or care afterward." Judas felt so bad for what he had done that he went back to those religious leaders and tried to give back the thirty pieces of silver that they had given Judas for betraying Jesus. They would not take back the money, so he went out and hung himself. He felt sorry for what he did. He tried to undo it. But he never did make himself right with the person he betrayed, Jesus.

CONCLUSION

THE ULTIMATE ENDGAME OF YOUR CHRISTIAN LIFE IS Christlikeness. Success in the spiritual battle means you don't merely settle for a bit of relief from oppression. It requires you to run after the fullness of the nature of Christ for every aspect of your life. Your objective is a soul that conforms to the righteousness of Jesus and displaces every area that the domain of darkness once occupied. Doing so not only protects you, it establishes your victory.

Your adversary wants to occupy any unsanctified thoughts and attitudes. The energy you expend to hide your sins actually protects the enemy's access to your life. Everything has to be brought into the light to dismantle any home the enemy has made within your thoughts and attitudes or you will be fighting a futile battle. If you are only trying to do as little as you can to live a "normal" life, you've missed what God is after. You've also been deceived into thinking that settling for an ordinary Christian existence, one which allows for a measure of compromise, will be enough to get the enemy off your back.

Only the nature of Christ in your life will bring you true rest and security, a place of immunity. God's plan for you to discover a continually overcoming life is to pursue the nature of Jesus. All that you go through ultimately brings you to that end. You aren't always aware of areas in your life that are in opposition to God when things are going your way. Times of struggle exert pressure that reveals your heart and gives God a chance to bring your inner man into holy alignment.

God doesn't rest until the nature of Christ is formed in you (Rom. 8:29). Fulfilling your destiny requires it. It brings you a peace that becomes a weapon as you face every circumstance. It positions you to be immovable so you can stand in victory. Your adversary isn't afraid of you, but he trembles at Christ in you! Submission to His rule gives you great authority for overcoming and conquering. The great news is that God gives you great grace for this journey! He is and always will be your source of strength!

Appendix A

PRAYERS TO PRAY

Prayer to Renounce Habitual Sin

Lord, I renounce the use of my body as an instrument of unrighteousness.

I acknowledge that I have given in to fleshly lusts that wage war against my soul.

I confess that I have willfully chosen to rebel against You and Your Word.

I repent of my willful disobedience.

I confess my sinful habit of _____ .

Thank You for Your forgiveness.

I receive the cleansing in my mind and body.

I declare that sin will not be my master, for in Christ I am now prone to righteousness.

I receive the grace to obey You and resist temptation.

Thank You that You love me unconditionally.

Thank You for setting me free.

I choose to follow You in obedience.

Prayer to Renounce Sexual Perversion and Pornography

I break all attachments to lust, perversion, fantasy, and sexual immorality.

I repent for viewing pornography for sexual stimulation, satisfaction, comfort, and escape.

I repent for any addiction of reading or viewing that captures my emotions in fantasy.

I confess that I have committed adultery in my heart.

I confess every act of sexual perversion with my body.

Cleanse me from the shame, humiliation, and filthiness that have clung to me from my defilement.

Cancel and cleanse my mind of wrongful images and wash my heart, returning it to purity.

I commit myself to see others as God's valuable creation and will give them the honor that God does.

I commit my mind, imagination, and emotions to You, my Lord.

I choose to dwell on things that are true, noble, right, and pure (Phil. 4:8).

Prayer to Renounce Involvement in Occult or Cult Practices

In Jesus' name, I renounce any involvement in _____ (name the occult or the cultic practice).

I renounce _____ (list the practices you participated in).

*I ask You, God, to forgive me for worshiping
other gods.*

I declare that Jesus is the way, the truth, and the life.

No one comes to the Father but through Jesus.

I declare that Jesus is Lord of all.

I will worship God and Him alone.

Substance Abuse Prayer

*I confess that I have misused _____ (alcohol,
tobacco, food, prescription or street drugs) for the
purpose of _____ (pleasure, to escape reality,
or to cope with difficult situations).*

*I repent for ensnaring myself and becoming a slave to
substances and allowing evil powers to rule over me.*

*I renounce any demonic connection or influence in my
life through my misuse of _____ .*

*Forgive me for abusing my body and quenching the
Holy Spirit.*

*I commit myself to no longer yield to _____,
but to yield to the Holy Spirit.*

*I admit my responsibility for damaging
my relationships.*

*I ask You to help those I have hurt, to heal each one, to
strengthen, restore, and bless them.*

*I take back dominion over my life that I have given
over to demonic influence.*

Heavenly Father, fill me afresh with Your Holy Spirit.

Breaking Generational Curses and Receiving Generational Blessings

General Generational Prayer

> *Heavenly Father, according to my covenant with*
> *You, I ask You to open the books of my past of every*
> *covenant made, which my forefathers entered into*
> *on my behalf that is giving protection to the demonic*
> *around me. Look at these, heavenly Father, and see if*
> *any of these are not absolutely righteous and just, and*
> *if not, then annul them and release the affliction of the*
> *demonic off of me. For those covenants that originate*
> *from You that are righteous and just, I receive the*
> *fullness of my ancestral blessings.*

Specific Generation Prayer

(The following prayer can be prayed repetitiously over each generation. Exodus 20:5 and Numbers 14:18 go to the third and fourth generations, so you can start with the fourth generation and then move to the third generation and so on until you get to your descendants.)

> *In the name of Jesus,*
> *I declare the blood of Jesus to stand between me and*
> *the _____ generation as a wall of separation.*
> *I cancel every assignment of darkness and remove*
> *every right of the demonic to afflict me because of the*
> *sin of that generation.*
> *I call to me my righteous inheritance and the blessings*
> *of the _____ generation.*

- Great-great-grandparents—fourth
- Great-grandparents—third
- Grandparents—second
- Parents—first
- Children/descendants

Prayer to Break Off Word Curses

In the name of Jesus I break every curse of words against me.

I take every word captive that has been spoken over me...and that I spoke over myself.

I break the power of those curses from hell.

I cancel every assignment of darkness.

I cast them to the ground and I call blessing to fall on me in their place.

I take back every curse I have spoken against another.

I cast those words down to the ground.

I return a blessing on those whom I have cursed.

Jesus took my cursing so I can live in blessing.

Forgiveness Prayer

In the name of Jesus, I choose to forgive as I have been forgiven.

I now choose to forgive _____.

I release any right I have retained to bring revenge against them.

*I release them from my hands and place them into
Your hands, Jesus, my Just Judge.*

*I break every curse I have spoken against them and I
call forth a blessing toward them in return.*

Thank You, Jesus, for giving me the grace to forgive.

Typical Breaking of Soul Tie Prayer

*In the authority of Jesus, I plead the blood of Jesus to
stand between me and _____ and separate
the "one flesh" union.*

*I send back to him/her everything that I have taken
from him/her when I became "one flesh" with him/her.*

*I call back to me everything that I gave in this "one
flesh" union.*

*I declare the blood of Jesus to be a wall of separation
between us.*

Thank You, Jesus, for restoring my soul.

Fear Bond Prayer

I will live in perfect love that casts out all fear.

I cast off the yoke of domination.

*I now choose to forgive _____ for their sin
against me and their oppression over me.*

I break off the power of their words over me.

I break the victim spirit off of me.

I rebuke the fear of man I have lived under.

*I cancel my bond to them declaring the blood of Jesus
as a wall between us.*

I take back my true identity.

I will not live under oppression.

I will receive my Father's love.

I am now free to live and to love.

The Spirit of Religion

In the name of Jesus I renounce every spirit of religion and every work of darkness connected with it.

I repent for allowing myself to be led by any spirit other than the Holy Spirit.

I renounce all forms of legalism, traditions of man, and participation in dead works.

I repent of my hypocrisy, pride, and arrogance.

I repent of relying on my own works and self-righteousness to find favor in the sight of God and man.

I repent of relying on my own intellect rather than your Holy Spirit and for inappropriately using scripture as a weapon to bring harm to other saints.

Forgive me for my false judgments, criticism, gossip, jealousy, covetousness, anger, and hardness of heart.

Forgive me for slandering and persecuting those who are moving in the Holy Spirit and for attributing the works of the Holy Spirit to the devil.

I renounce any belief that portrays You, Lord, as distant and judgmental and I receive the fullness of Your love, compassion, mercy, and grace.

I choose to embrace all of the aspects of Your true character and to know You intimately.

I choose to no longer partner with the same spirit that killed Jesus and that continues to attempt to kill the work of the Holy Spirit today.

I choose to come into agreement with God my Father, with Jesus Christ, and with the Holy Spirit.

Appendix B

LIES THAT PEOPLE BELIEVE

- I was not wanted.
- I can't do anything right.
- I hate myself.
- I just don't like people.
- I don't like myself.
- Everything I touch turns out bad.
- I always feel ashamed.
- I deserve a crappy life.
- I don't deserve to be free.
- I'm not good enough to find a spouse.
- I'm not able to make friends.
- I'm unlovable.
- I can't be a good parent.
- Life has no purpose for me.
- God is waiting for a moment that He can drop the hammer on me.
- God hates me.
- God despises me.

- I am God's reject.

- Everyone else has favor except me.

- I am always afraid.

- I can't control my fear.

- I can't control my anger.

- I'm a loser.

- I don't feel important.

- God likes others more than me.

- I have no self-control.

- I am doomed to fail.

- I can't have victory.

- The devil has power over me.

- I can't tell the truth.

- A lie is easier than the truth.

- I feel rejected.

- I'm unwanted.

- I have to push others down so I can feel better about myself.

- My value is threatened when others around me are esteemed.

Appendix C

A PARTIAL LIST OF TRUTHS ABOUT GOD THE FATHER, JESUS THE SON, AND THE HOLY SPIRIT

- There is only one true and living God (1 Cor. 8:6; Eph. 4:6; 1 Tim. 2:5).

- Jesus Christ is the Christ, the only way to the Father (John 14:6).

- Jesus destroyed the works of the devil (1 John 3:8).

- Jesus disarmed the rulers and authorities, having triumphed over them through His shed blood on the cross (Col 2:14-15).

- Jesus rendered the devil powerless and sets people free (Heb. 2:15).

- Jesus now has all authority in heaven and on earth (Matt. 28:18).

- He has authority over the world (John 16:33).

- Jesus is seated at the right hand of the Father far above all rule, all power, all authority, and above every name that is named, not only in this age, but also in the one to come (Eph. 1:20-21).

- Everything is in subjection under Jesus' feet (Eph. 1:22).

- God will never leave me nor forsake me (Heb. 13:5).

- God's love is unfailing (Jer. 31:3).

- God's character is unchangeable (Num. 23:19; James 1:17; Heb. 13:5).

- God's power is unlimited (Jer. 32:17; Luke 1:37; Matt. 19:26).

- God is unequalled (Isa. 40:13-25).

- God is faithful (Deut. 7:9; Ps. 89:1-8).

- God is true and truth (John 14:6; Ps. 31:5; Titus 1:1-2).

- God is good (Ps. 25:8; 34:8; Mark 10:18).

- God abounds in goodness (Ps. 31:19; 52:1; Rom. 11:22).

- God is merciful (Deut. 4:31; Ps. 103:8-17; Dan. 9:9; Heb. 2:17).

- God is love (John 3:16; Rom. 5:8; 1 John 4:8,16).

- God is light (1 John 1:5).

- God is all knowing (1 John 3:20).

- God is everywhere (Ps. 139:7-12).

- God is without limit (1 Kings 8:27).

Appendix D

COMMON TRUTHS ABOUT OUR IDENTITY IN CHRIST

- I am a child of God (John 1:12).

- I am Jesus' friend (John 15:15).

- I am no longer a slave but a son/daughter (Gal. 4:5-7).

- I have been adopted as son/daughter (Rom. 8:15: Eph. 1:5).

- I am a son/daughter of God; God is spiritually my Father (Rom. 8:14-15; Gal. 3:26; 4:6).

- I am an heir of God because I am a son/daughter of God (Gal. 4:6-7).

- I am a joint heir with Christ, sharing His inheritance with Him (Rom. 8:17).

- I am a member of Christ's Body (1 Cor. 12:27; Eph. 5:30).

- I am saved by grace through faith and not of my works (Eph. 2:8-9).

- Jesus delivered me from the domain of darkness and transferred me to His Kingdom (Col. 1:13).

- I have been forgiven of all my sin (Col. 2:13).

- I am enslaved to God (Rom. 6:22).

- I am a temple—a dwelling place—of God. His Spirit and His life dwells in me (1 Cor. 3:16; 6:19).

- I am a citizen of heaven (Phil. 3:20).

- I am a fellow citizen with the rest of God's family (Eph. 2:19).

- I am an alien and stranger to this world in which I temporarily live (1 Pet. 2:11).

- I am hidden with Christ in God (Col. 3:3).

- I am chosen of God, holy and dearly loved (Col. 3:12; 1 Thess. 1:4).

- I am a partaker of Christ; I share in His life (Heb. 3:14).

- I am one of God's living stones, being built up in Christ as a spiritual house (1 Pet. 2:5).

- I have been bought with a price. I belong to God (1 Cor. 6:20).

- I am a new creature, the old is gone, the new has come (2 Cor. 5:17).

- Sin is no longer my master (Rom. 6:14).

- I have been freed from sin (Rom. 6:18).

- I am prone to do righteousness (Rom. 6:18).

- I am a saint (1 Cor. 1:2; Eph. 1:1; Phil. 1:1; Col. 1:2).

- I am a slave of righteousness (Rom. 6:18).

- I am righteous and holy (Eph. 4:24).

- I am a son of light and not of darkness (1 Thess. 5:5).

- I am a member of a chosen race, a royal priesthood, a holy nation, a people for God's own possession (1 Pet. 2:9-10).

- I have been justified (Rom. 5:1).

- I have direct access to God through the Holy Spirit (Eph. 2:18).

- I have been redeemed and forgiven of all my sins (Col. 1:14).

- I am complete in Christ (Col. 2:10).

- I am free from condemnation (Rom. 8:1-2).

- I have been established, anointed, and sealed by God (2 Cor. 1:21-22).

- I am united to the Lord and am one spirit with Him (1 Cor. 6:17).

- I died with Christ (Rom. 6:5,8).

- I was crucified with Christ (Gal. 2:20; Rom 6:6).

- I was buried with Christ (Rom. 6:4).

- I rose with Christ (Rom. 6:5).

- I am seated with Jesus in the heavenlies (Eph. 2:6).

- I can resist the devil and he will flee from me (James 4:7).

- God has given me spiritual weapons and spiritual armor (Eph. 6:12-18).

- I can stand firm against the schemes of the enemy (Eph. 6:11).

- I can be strong in the Lord and the strength of His might (Eph. 6:10).

- I have victory through Christ (1 Cor. 15:57).

- I am more than a conqueror (Rom. 8:37).

- I have overcome the world (1 John 5:4).

- My weapons are divinely powerful to tear down the strongholds of darkness (2 Cor. 10:3-4).

- Greater is He who is in me than he who is in the world (1 John 4:4).

- I have been given authority over the powers of the enemy and the enemy cannot injure me (Luke 10:19).

- I have not been given a spirit of fear but of power, love, and a sound mind (2 Tim. 1:7).

- I am born of God and the evil one cannot touch me (1 John 5:18).

- I can find grace and mercy in time of need (Heb. 4:16).

- I am a branch of the true vine, a channel of His life (John 15:1,5).

- I have been chosen and appointed to bear fruit (John 15:16).

- I am assured that all things work together for good (Rom. 8:28).

- I am free from any condemning charges against me (Rom. 8:31-34).

- I cannot be separated from the love of God (Rom. 8:35-38).

- I can do all things through Christ who strengthens me (Phil. 4:13).

- I am confident that the good work God has begun in me will be perfected (Phil. 1:6).

- I am a minister of reconciliation for God (2 Cor. 5:17-21).

- I am the salt of the earth (Matt. 5:13).

- I am the light of the world (Matt. 5:14).

- I am God's coworker (1 Cor. 3:9; 2 Cor. 6:1).

- I have confidence to approach the throne of grace (Heb. 4:16).

- I can always find mercy and grace to help in time of need (Heb. 4:16).

- I may approach God with freedom and confidence (Eph. 3:12).

- I am never left alone nor forsaken (Heb. 13:5).

- I am chosen and appointed by Christ to bear His fruit (John 15:16).

- I am reconciled to God and am a minister of reconciliation (2 Cor. 5:18-19).

- I am God's workmanship, created to do His works (Eph. 2:10).

- I am an expression of the life of Christ because He is my life (Col. 3:4).

- I am a holy partaker of a heavenly calling (Heb. 3:1).

- I am part of the true vine, a channel of Christ's life (John 15:1,5).

Appendix E

EXAMPLES OF FALSE IDENTITIES PEOPLE EMBRACE

* I am a victim.

* I am a worrier.

* I am overbearing.

* I am a controlling person.

* I am a manipulating person.

* I am an angry person.

* I am a disoriented, confused person.

* I'm a needy person.

* I'm rebellious.

* I always feel judged.

* I am a liar.

* I'm a negative person.

* I'm a pervert.

* I'm a judgmental person.

* I'm a bitter person.

- I'm a distrusting person. (I can't trust others.)

- I'm a distrustful person. (I can't be trusted.)

- I'm a closed person.

- I'm an unfriendly person.

- I'm a fearful person.

- I am a coward.

- I'm a failure.

- I live in self-condemnation.

Appendix F

How to Do a Character Bible Study

What is the righteous stronghold that you need to pursue? You may have more than one, but start with the one that you might consider the primary one. If you don't know the righteous stronghold or you are unclear, you can list the negative one and search out the opposite character traits to discover the one you want to pursue.

1. *Define the righteous stronghold.*

Begin by listing what you think is the righteous stronghold you want to put into your life. To dig into what the Bible may say about this, it is good to begin with a broad search and see all the related words. Look this word up in a dictionary and see all the definitions, the synonyms, and antonyms. Antonyms can give you key words to study that might point to verses to address the negative trait and build the positive trait. For example, if you were focusing on a stronghold of faithfulness or faith, the opposite would be unfaithfulness, doubt, apathy, and fear. Those opposites may provide scriptures that speak to tearing those negative traits down or keys to overcoming them. If you don't have a positive trait to pursue but only a negative trait you are ridding yourself of, search the antonyms of the synonyms of the negative trait and you may find the stronghold of righteousness that you want to give attention to. Word-processing programs like Microsoft Word often have a feature in their tools category where you can do it.

If you have access to a Bible dictionary or word study book (and there are some free ones online) you can see how this is defined in scripture. This could also help you see how this might be different than just looking at it as it is being used in everyday language.

For example, if you were studying the quality meekness, you will run across a common definition that it is a quality of humility and gentleness toward others. If you look it up in the original Greek, you will see that it actually refers to power at your disposal but choosing restraint. The word was used to describe the training of valuable horses in which they were brought under submission to their masters. A stallion would still have all the power and strength of its wild days but was now under the master's control. *Meekness,* therefore, was not *weakness.* As a Christian quality, meekness is strength that is in submission to Jesus Christ.

- List the stronghold(s) you are wanting to pursue.
- List any definitions you find for the word (dictionary, Bible dictionary, word study book).
- List the synonyms you find.
- List any antonyms.

2. Find some scriptures relating to the character and look for any cross-references.

Now it is time to get deeper into the Word of God. A great place to begin is to look in a topical Bible like *Nave's Topical Bible* and look up that character and read the verses related to that topic. Verses are listed topically so they may not have the exact word in them. If any verses stand out to you, look them up in context and see if there are any other verses related to it. Some Bibles have cross-references that may point to relevant verses. Scripture is still the best interpreter of scripture. Use a concordance to find all the verses that you can on this trait. *Strong's Concordance* is a classic and relatively cheap, plus there are free versions online. Doing a word search on a Bible program will do the same to bring up all the verses where that word is used. You could even do that on a Bible program on your smartphone using a word search feature. Some concordances may even define those words, giving you a biblical definition.

As you look at these verses, ask relevant questions. Asking questions of the verses as you read them will help you probe those verses and pull out deeper meaning that you might miss in just reading them. Be sure and record those verses and whatever insight you gain from them. Write out your observations. Here is a starter list of questions but you might want to add to it.

- What benefit can this trait bring you?

- What are some bad consequences this trait can bring you (if it's a negative trait)?

- What are some benefits this trait can bring to others?

- What are some bad consequences this trait can bring to others (if it's a negative trait)?

- Is there any promise from God related to this trait?

- Is there any warning or judgment related to this trait (if it's a negative trait)?

- Is there any command related to this trait?

- What factors produce this trait?

- Did Jesus have anything to say about this quality? What did He say?

- What writer talked about this quality the most?

- Is this trait symbolized by anything in scripture? Is that significant and why?

- Is this trait listed with a group of qualities? What is the relationship between them? What does that suggest?

- What scriptures tell us directly what God thinks of this trait?

To sum up this step:

- Look up the words in a topical Bible, a concordance, or search for them in a Bible program.

- Read the verses and see which ones you want to include and list them.

- List the references of the relevant verses and write a brief summary of what the verse is saying. Put a mark or star beside the ones that are most important.

- Look at the most significant verses that you marked and start with those.

- Ask the questions of the verses to dig deeper.

- What scriptures clearly spells out what God thinks of this trait?

3. *Write out a summary of what you have learned.*

Step two can be very time consuming but well worth the investment of your time. After looking at your notes of the verses you picked out and the observations and insights you gained after asking those questions, write out a summary of what you have learned. List any lessons or principles you learned. You may want to rephrase or paraphrase a few key verses.

If you have any difficulties with any of the verses, you should document those as well. Write down the questions you would like to see answered later on. This might be something that you would choose to study at a later date.

4. *Find and study a biblical person who demonstrated that trait.*

It is always helpful to look at any who modeled this character so you can glean from their life. See if you can find at least one person, preferably more if possible, who showed this character quality in his or her life. Sometimes we learn from the person whose life demonstrated the opposite of what we want and can look at their life to see what we want to avoid. Briefly describe this quality in their life and write down the scriptures that refer to it. You can ask these questions that are geared to a positive character trait you are studying.

- What shows this quality in his/her life?
- How did this quality affect his/her life?
- Did the quality help or hinder his/her growth to maturity? How?
- What results did it produce in his/her life?
- What happened in their life to produce this trait?
- What happened in their life to hinder this trait?

5. *Ask yourself what you can do (from what you have learned) to put this quality into your own personal life.*

Begin thinking of a current area in your own life where God wants to work out this particular character quality. This can either be a situation or an interpersonal relationship. If it is a situation, begin to anticipate, in advance, what you will do when the situation arises. If it is a relationship, determine ahead of time how you will respond in your interactions with that person. Begin to look for opportunities to work on that character trait in your relationships with that person or persons. Your goal is to have more mature relationships.

6. *Plan a specific project.*

This is a practical part of the application and is actually working out step five. Begin thinking of a project that you will work on to build this positive trait in your life. Write out a plan, do it, and then evaluate it. Be specific and write down where you have succeeded and where you might have failed. Make adjustments to your plan and go at it again.

For example, let's say that you are working on building a stronghold of love or compassion. You might need a little help in getting a "jump start" in loving with God's love. You might want to warm up to this idea with a little less threatening of an exercise. Start by thinking of a person whom you can love, but who is not in the habit of loving you. It does not require much to love when you are loved, so choose someone with whom you can practice loving with God's love, even if love is not returned. Start with a person with whom you don't have an issue. That person is much safer than trying to love the one who actively hates you. Start doing acts of kindness without expecting something in return to demonstrate God's love.

The objective is to begin to establish a habit of loving in God's way, training your heart to love.

God often builds character in our lives by putting us in situations where we are tempted to do the opposite. God will give you an opportunity to exercise what you have learned about that particular trait.

Repeat the biblical study on other godly strongholds that you need to pursue.

Appendix G

CREATING A UNIQUE PERSONAL IDENTITY STATEMENT

HAVING LOOKED AT THE TRUTHS OF YOUR TRUE IDENTITY and having looked at the truths of the godly strongholds you discovered, it is time to put together an identity statement. This identity statement should be your own unique statement of who you are. Include the general truths of who you are in Christ that really need emphasizing in your life. Include truths that disable your false identity and promote your true identity. Say it over yourself every day and let the truth of God's Word sink into your spirit. When our words are in agreement with what God says about us, they release the grace for the fulfillment of the assignments of heaven, empowering the angels as we unleash our authority to bind and loose them toward the purposes of God. That is what an identity statement does when it becomes your own and is declared over you regularly. It becomes a pool of truth that the Holy Spirit can bring to your mind the moment you need it.

An identity statement would be like:

I am God's wonderful creation.

Throughout the ages God was thinking about me.

He planned me before I was born.

He had written in His book the plans for my life.

His plans for me are for prosperity and not for calamity,

To give me a future and a hope.

He loves me.

He sent His Son to die in my place.

He redeemed me to bring me into my destiny.

I've been adopted into God's family.

I am loved by my heavenly Papa.

He doesn't withhold good from me.

He delights to shower blessing over me.

He has given me everything I need to succeed and overcome.

All grace abounds toward me so I will have enough for every good work.

Nothing is impossible for God.

I **can** do all things through Christ,

Because greater is He who is in me than he who is in the world.

This is very general one but you can see that it speaks into a person's identity. It isn't so long that it will be frustrating. It isn't too short not to be challenging. It should be a statement regarding what God is teaching you about you. You take the truths of your true identity and you jot down the things you need to remind yourself of. Here are a few more examples of some who have created their identity statement.

I used to live what I am not, but that will never happen again. I am as He is. I will be the full reflection of my Papa, my King. I am His and He is mine and nothing can separate me from that. Though winds will blow and storms will rage, His grace always beckons me to come into His peace. And there I will reside. His light is so radiant that not a speck of darkness can settle on me, for it quickly burns away under His brilliance within me. His glory is so alluring, I am compelled to run after every opportunity to manifest His love and power. His Word is my breath and my life that I can never depart from. His Holy Spirit is my resting place, where I go for comfort, truth, and the knowledge of Christ. I am a lover of His people, a defender of the weak, a dispenser of His riches, and my joy overflows. I grow and He prunes. I say ouch. Then I notice the blossoms budding from the place just pruned, and I thank Him for His touch that keeps bringing me from glory to glory. I love Him more than I can say. I am undone by His love.

I was chosen before time to be a light in the earth for the purpose He destined for me. I heard Him call my name and speak my destiny into my being. I was formed in secret and created unique, set apart in the sight of God. I am fearfully and wonderfully made.

I am a blood-bought daughter of the King of Glory. Adopted into His family; joint heir with Christ. I am complete in Him. He resides in me and I reside with Him in Heaven. I cannot be separated from His love. I am a citizen of Heaven and an ambassador to earth.

I have full access to the throne of God and am welcomed to stand face to face with my Papa. I have been created to walk out a unique destiny that only I can fulfill. I am the daughter of the King; a priestess of the Most High God; a warrior princess loved and cherished by my heavenly Father. I have been established, anointed, and sealed by God. I am His and He is mine. I stand in awe of Him, who loves me.

I walk in grace, compassion, and mercy. I am the salt and the light on the earth, a branch of the True Vine. I have been chosen to bear fruit. I speak healing, wholeness, shalom. I am the apple of my Father's eye, His favorite, His treasure. I am righteous and holy. I am free.

The Spirit of power and love is at work in me. I am courageous with my love. I am powerful to control myself no matter what. I am the bearer of exceptional graces. I am the bearer of the grace of mercy, compassion. I wear the grace of miracles in everything. I am the bearer of the grace of God's unlimited healing power. I am a deliverer; the light of the Gospel shines in my mind. I will bless those around me both physically and spiritually. I am more than a conqueror through Him who loves me. I am not under the control and dominion of darkness, but I am in the Kingdom of light. I can press on toward the goal to win the prize for which God has called me heavenward in Christ Jesus. I am loved with an intense love. I am sufficient in Christ's sufficiency.

I am His favored child. I am a beloved friend of God seated in heavenly places by His right hand, a hand's breadth away. He reaches down and takes my hand. I stand close to Him. He reaches out to me as I reach out to Him. Before He left this earth, Jesus prayed for me. He likes to dance with me. I am all things in Christ who strengthens me: a dancer, a lover, and a speaker. I am a revelator. As Christ came to reveal the Father, I seek to reveal Him to the world. I am a divine, holy, righteous child. I have His witness inside of me. I am His instrument; I resonate in the song He sings over me. Nothing and no one, in this world or any realm, can separate me from Him.

About Rodney Hogue

Dr. Rodney Hogue has been in full-time ministry since 1977. He pastored over 32 years on the west coast in Washington state and California, his last being 23 years at Community of Grace in Hayward, California. Rodney now ministers itinerantly, equipping believers nationally and internationally to walk out their identity and expand God's Kingdom, which includes demonstrating the Kingdom of God with power.

Made in United States
Troutdale, OR
04/24/2024